The Prophet
(Peace Be Upon Him)

Book #1

Ibn Kathir

Copyright

Kathir

Noaha

Editor: Al-Imam Ahmad

Al-Azhar Publications

Good Books

Search by **ISBN** to buy the correct book

Stories of the Prophets	ISBN: 9781643543888
Story of the Holy Prophet	ISBN: 9781643544267
The Noble Quran (Arabic)	ISBN: 9781643543994
Koran (English: Easy to Read)	ISBN: 9781643540924
Life in al-Barzakh: Life after Death	ISBN: 9781643544144
The Heavenly Dispute	ISBN: 9781643544168
The Journey of the Strangers	ISBN: 9781643544175
Disciplining the Soul	ISBN: 9781643544151

ISBN: 9781643544120

Diseases of the Hearts & Cures	ISBN 9781643544106
The Friends of Allah	ISBN: 9781643544236
The Path to Guidance	ISBN: 9781643544052
Miracles of the Prophet	ISBN: 9781643544038
Seerah of Prophet Muhammad	ISBN: 9781643543222
Book on Islam and Marriage	ISBN: 9781073877140
The Spiritual Cure	ISBN: 9781643544212
Great Women of Islam	ISBN: 9781643543758
Stories of the Koran	ISBN: 9781095900796
The Purification of the Soul	ISBN: 9781643541389
Al-Fawaid: Wise Sayings	ISBN: 9781727812718
The Book of Hajj	ISBN: 9781072243335

40 Hadith Qudsi	ISBN: 9781070655949
40 Hadith Nawawi	ISBN: 9781070547428
The Legacy of the Prophet	ISBN: 9781080249343
The Ideal Muslim Woman	ISBN: 9781643543192
The Soul's Journey after Death	ISBN: 9781643541365
Khalid Bin Al-Waleed	ISBN: 9781643543420
The Islamic View of Jesus	ISBN: 978164354335
Don't Be Sad	ISBN: 9781643543451
Ota Benga	ISBN: 9798698096665

The Prophet
(Peace and Blessings Be Upon Him)

Without any doubts, the biography of the Prophet (Peace and Blessings be Upon Him) is authentic, truthful and complete. Prophet Muhammad (peace be upon him) was an exemplary man of intelligent mind and faultless vision. He was called "the truthful and the trustworthy" long before he became the Messenger of Allah (peace and blessings be upon him). In view of this, an entire chapter is here presented about the Arab tribes prior to Islam as well as the environment that enwrapped the Prophet's mission.

The Arabian Peninsula:

Linguistically, the word "Arab" means deserts and waste barren land that is waterless and treeless. Ever since the dawn of time, the Arabian Peninsula and its people have been called Arab.

The Arabian Peninsula is enclosed in the west by Sinai and the Red Sea, in the east by the Arabian Gulf, in the south by the Arabian Sea, which is an extension of the Indian Ocean, and in the north by old Syria and part of Iraq.

Geographically, the Arabian Peninsula includes Kuwait, Oman, Qatar, Saudi Arabia, the United Arab Emirates (UAE), and Yemen, as well as the southern portions of Iraq and Jordan. The biggest of these is Saudi Arabia. The Peninsula, plus Bahrain, the Socotra Archipelago, and other nearby islands form a geopolitical region called Arabia. Throughout history, thanks to its geographical position, the Arabian Peninsula has always maintained great importance. Considering its climate, which is mostly deserts, it has rendered it inaccessible to invaders. Therefore, it allowed its people complete liberty and independence through the many centuries, despite the presence of two neighboring great empires.

The Arab Tribes:

Arab kinfolks have been divided according to lineage into three groups:

Perishing Arabs: The ancient Arabs, of whose history little is known, and of whom were 'Ad, Thamûd, Tasam, Jadis, Emlaq, and others.

Pure Arabs: Who originated from the progeny of Ya'rub bin Yashjub bin Qahtan. They were also called Qahtanian Arabs.

Arabized Arabs: Who originated from the progeny of Ishmael. They were also called 'Adnanian Arabs.

The pure Arabs – the people of Qahtan – originally lived in Yemen and comprised many tribes, two of which were very famous:

1. Himyar: The most famous of whose septs were Zaid Al-Jamhur, Quda'a and Sakasic.

2. Kahlan: The most famous of whose septs were Hamdan, Anmar, Tai', Mudhhij, Kinda, Lakhm, Judham, Azd, Aws, Khazraj and the descendants of Jafna — the kings of old Syria.

Kahlan septs emigrated from Yemen to dwell in the different parts of the Arabian Peninsula prior to the Great Flood (Sail Al-'Arim of Ma'rib Dam), due to the failure of trade under the Roman pressure and domain on both sea and land trade routes following Roman occupation of Egypt and Syria.

Naturally enough, the competition between Kahlan and Himyar led to the evacuation of the first and the settlement of the second in Yemen.

1. Azd: Who, under the leadership of 'Imran bin 'Amr Muzaiqbâ', wandered in Yemen, sent pioneers and finally headed northwards. Details of their emigration can be summed up as follows:

2. Tha'labah bin 'Amr left his tribe Al-Azd for Hijaz and dwelt between Tha'labiyah and Dhi Qar.

When he gained strength, he headed for Madinah where he stayed. Of his seed are Aws and Khazraj, sons of Haritha bin Tha'labah.

Haritha bin 'Amr, known as Khuza'a, wandered with his folks in Hijaz until they came to Mar Az- Zahran. Later, they conquered the Haram, and settled in Makkah after having driven away its people, the tribe of Jurhum.

'Imran bin 'Amr and his folks went to 'Oman where they established the tribe of Azd whose children inhabited Tihama and were known as Azd-of-Shanu'a.

Jafna bin 'Amr and his family, headed for Syria where he settled and initiated the kingdom of Ghassan who was so named after a spring of water, in Hijaz, where they stopped on their way to Syria.

Lakhm and Judham: Of whom was Nasr bin Rabi'a, father of Manadhira, Kings of Heerah.

Banu Tai': Who also emigrated northwards to settle by the so- called Aja and Salma Mountains which were consequently named as Tai' Mountains.

Kinda: Who dwelt in Bahrain but were expelled to Hadramout and Najd where they instituted a powerful government but not for long, for the whole tribe soon faded away.

Another tribe of Himyar, known as Quda'a, also left Yemen and dwelt in Samawa semi-desert on the borders of Iraq.

The Arabized Arabs go back in ancestry to their great grandfather Abraham (Peace be upon him) from a town called "Ar" near Kufa on the west bank of the Euphrates in Iraq. Excavations brought to light great details of the town, Abraham's family, and the prevalent religions and social circumstances.

It is known that Abraham (Peace be upon him) left Ar for Harran and then for Palestine, which he made headquarters for his Message. He wandered all over the area. When he went to Egypt, the Pharaoh tried to do evil to his wife Sarah, but Allâh saved her and the Pharaoh's wicked scheme recoiled on him. He thus came to realize her strong attachment to Allâh, and, in acknowledgment of her grace, the Pharaoh rendered his daughter Hagar at Sarah's service, but Sarah gave Hagar to Abraham as a wife.

Abraham returned to Palestine where Hagar gave birth to Ishmael. Sarah became so jealous of Hagar that she forced Abraham to send Hagar and her baby away to a plantless valley on a small hill in Hijaz, by the Sacred House, exposed to the wearing of floods coming right and left. He chose for them a place under a lofty tree above Zamzam near the upper side of the Mosque in Makkah where neither people nor water was available, and went back to Palestine leaving with his wife and baby a leather case with some dates and a pot of water. Not before long, they ran out of both food and water, but thanks to Allâh's favor water gushed forth to sustain them for some time. The whole story of Zamzam spring is already known to everybody.

Another Yemeni tribe – Jurhum the Second – came and lived in Makkah upon Hagar's permission, after being said to have lived in the valleys around Makkah. It is mentioned in the Sahih Al-Bukhari that this tribe came to Makkah before Ishmael was a young man while they had passed through that valley long before this event.

Abraham used to go to Makkah every now and then to see his wife and son. The number of these journeys is still unknown, but authentic historical resources spoke of four ones.

Allâh, the Sublime, stated in the Noble Qur'ân that He had Abraham see, in his dream, that he slaughtered his son Ishmael, and therefore Abraham stood up to fulfill His Order:

• "Then, when they had both submitted themselves (to the Will of Allâh), and he had laid him prostrate on his forehead (or on the side of his forehead for slaughtering); and We called out to him: "O Abraham! You have fulfilled the dream (vision)!" Verily! Thus do we reward the

Muhsinûn (good-doers, who perform good deeds totally for Allâh's sake only, without any show off or to gain praise or fame, etc. and do them in accordance to Allâh's Orders). Verily, that indeed was a manifest trial — and We ransomed him with a great sacrifice (i.e. a ram)" [37:103- 107]

فَلَمَّآ أَسْلَمَا وَتَلَّهُۥ لِلْجَبِينِ ۝

وَنَٰدَيْنَٰهُ أَن يَٰٓإِبْرَٰهِيمُ ۝

قَدْ صَدَّقْتَ ٱلرُّءْيَآ إِنَّا كَذَٰلِكَ نَجْزِى ٱلْمُحْسِنِينَ ۝

إِنَّ هَٰذَا لَهُوَ ٱلْبَلَٰٓؤُاْ ٱلْمُبِينُ ۝

وَفَدَيْنَٰهُ بِذِبْحٍ عَظِيمٍ ۝

It is mentioned in the Genesis that Ishmael was thirteen years older than his brother Ishaq. The sequence of the story of the sacrifice of Ishmael shows that it really happened before Ishaq's birth, and that Allâh's Promise to give Abraham another son, Ishaq, came after narration of the whole story.

This story spoke of one journey – at least – before Ishmael became a young man. Al-Bukhari, on the authority of Ibn 'Abbas, reported the other three journeys; a summary of which goes as follows:

When Ishmael became a young man, he learned Arabic at the hand of the tribe of Jurhum, who loved him with great admiration and gave him one of their women as a wife, soon after his mother died. Having wanted to see his wife and son again, Abraham came to Makkah, Ishmael's marriage, but he didn't find him at home. He asked Ishmael's wife about her husband and how they were doing. She complained of poverty, so he asked her to tell Ishmael to change his doorstep. Ishmael understood the message, divorced his wife and got married to the daughter of Mudad bin 'Amr, chief of the tribe of Jurhum.

Once more, Abraham came to see his son, but again didn't find him at home. He asked his new wife the same previous question, to which she thanked Allâh. Abraham asked her to tell Ishmael to keep his doorstep (i.e. to keep her as wife) and went back to Palestine.

A third time, Abraham came to Makkah to find Ishmael sharpening an arrow under a lofty tree near Zamzam. The meeting, after a very long journey of separation, was very touching for a father so affectionate and a so dutiful and righteous son. This time, father and son built Al-Ka'bah and raised its pillars, and Abraham, in compliance with Allâh's Commandment, called unto people to make pilgrimage to it.

By the grace of Allâh, Ishmael had twelve sons from the daughter of Mudad, whose names were Nabet, Qidar, Edbael, Mebsham, Mishma', Duma, Micha, Hudud, Yetma, Yetour, Nafis and Qidman, and who ultimately formed twelve tribes inhabiting Makkah and trading between Yemen, geographical Syria and Egypt. Later on, these tribes spread all over, and even outside, the peninsula. All their tidings went into oblivion except for the descendants of Nabet and Qidar.

The Nabeteans – sons of Nabet – established a flourishing civilization in the north of Hijaz, they instituted a powerful government which spread out its domain over all neighbouring tribes, and made Petra their capital.

Nobody dared challenge their authority until the Romans came and managed to eliminate their kingdom. After extensive research and painstaking investigation, Mr. Sulaiman An-Nadwi came to the conclusion that the Ghassanide kings, along with the Aws and Khazraj were not likely to be Qahtanians but rather Nabeteans.

Descendants of Qidar, the son of Ishmael, lived long in Makkah increasing in number, of them issued 'Adnan and son Ma'ad, to whom 'Adnanian Arabs traced back their ancestry. 'Adnan is the twenty-first grandfather in the series of the Prophetic ancestry. It was said that whenever Prophet Muhammad, peace be upon him, spoke of his ancestry he would stop at 'Adnan and say: "Genealogists tell lies" and did not go farther than him. A group of scholars, however, favoured the probability of going beyond 'Adnan attaching no significance to the aforementioned Prophetic Hadith. They went on to say that there were exactly forty fathers between 'Adnan and Abraham (Peace be upon them).

Nizar, Ma'ad's only son, had four sons who branched out into four great tribes; Eyad, Anmar, Rabi'a and Mudar. These last two sub-branched into several septs. Rabi'a fathered Asad, 'Anazah, 'Abdul Qais, and Wa'il's two sons (Bakr and Taghlib), Hanifa and many others.

Mudar tribes branched out into two great divisions: Qais 'Ailan bin Mudar and septs of Elias bin Mudar. Of Qais 'Ailan were the Banu Saleem, Banu Hawazin, and Banu Ghatafan of whom descended 'Abs, Zubyan, Ashja' and Ghani bin A'sur. Of Elias bin Mudar were Tamim bin Murra, Hudhail bin Mudrika, Banu Asad bin Khuzaimah and septs of Kinana bin Khuzaimah, of whom came Quraish, the descendants of Fahr bin Malik bin An-Nadr bin Kinana.

Quraish branched out into various tribes, the most famous of whom were Jumah, Sahm, 'Adi, Makhzum, Tayim, Zahra and the three septs of Qusai bin Kilab: 'Abdud-Dar bin Qusai, Asad bin 'Abdul 'Uzza bin Qusai and 'Abd Manaf bin Qusai.

'Abd Manaf branched out into four tribes: 'Abd Shams, Nawfal, Muttalib and Hashim. It is, however, from the family of Hashim that Allâh selected Prophet Muhammad bin 'Abdullah bin 'Abdul-Muttalib bin Hashim (Peace be upon him).

Prophet Muhammad (Peace be upon him) said: "Allâh selected Ishmael from the sons of Abraham, Kinana from the sons of Ishmael, Quraish from the sons of Kinana, Hashim from the sons of Quraish and He selected me from the sons of Hashim."

Al-'Abbas bin 'Abdul-Muttalib quoted the Messenger of Allâh (Peace be upon him) as saying: "Allâh created mankind and chose me from the best whereof, He chose the tribes and selected me from the best whereof; and He chose families and selected me from the best whereof. I am the very best in person and family."

Having increased in number, children of 'Adnan, in pursuit of pastures and water, spread out over various parts of Arabia. The tribe of 'Abdul Qais, together with some septs of Bakr bin Wa'il and Tamim, emigrated to Bahrain where they dwelt.

Banu Hanifa bin Sa'b bin Ali bin Bakr went to settle in Hijr, the capital of Yamama. All the tribes of Bakr bin Wa'il lived in an area of land which included Yamama, Bahrain, Saif Kazima, the sea shore, the outer borders of Iraq, Ablah and Hait.

Most of the tribe of Taghlib lived in the Euphrates area while some of them lived with Bakr. Banu Tamim lived in Basra semi-desert. Banu Saleem lived in the vicinity of Madinah on the land stretching from Wadi Al-Qura to Khaibar onwards to the eastern mountains to Harrah.

Thaqif dwelt in Ta'if and Hawazin east of Makkah near Autas on the road from Makkah to Basra. Banu Asad lived on the land east of Taimâ' and west of Kufa, while family of Tai' lived between Banu Asad and Taimâ'. They were five-day-walk far from Kufa. Zubyan inhabited the plot of land between Taimâ' and Hawran.

Some septs of Kinana lived in Tihama, while septs of Quraish dwelt in Makkah and its suburbs. Quraish remained completely disunited until Qusai bin Kilab managed to rally their ranks on honourable terms attaching major prominence to their status and importance.

RULERSHIP AND PRINCESHIP AMONG THE ARABS

When talking about the Arabs before Islam, we deem it necessary to draw a mini-picture of the history of rulership, princeship, sectarianism and the religious dominations of the Arabs, so as to facilitate the understanding of emergent circumstances when Islam appeared.

When the sun of Islam rose, rulers of Arabia were of two kinds: crowned kings, who were in fact not independent; and heads of tribes and clans, who enjoyed the same authorities and privileges possessed by crowned kings and were mostly independent, though some of whom could have shown some kind of submission to a crowned king. The crowned kings were only those of Yemen, Heerah and Ghassan. All other rulers of Arabia were non-crowned.

RULERSHIP IN YEMEN:

The folks of Sheba were one of the oldest nations of the pure Arabs, who lived in Yemen. Excavations at "Or" brought to light their existence twenty five centuries B.C. Their civilization flourished, and their domain spread eleven centuries B.C. It is possible to divide their ages according to the following estimation:

1. The centuries before 650 B.C., during which their kings were called "Makrib Sheba". Their capital was "Sarwah", also known as "Khriba", whose ruins lie in a spot, a day's walk from the western side of "Ma'rib". During this period, they started building the "Dam of Ma'rib" which had great importance in the history of Yemen. Sheba was also said to have had so great a domain that they had colonies inside and outside Arabia.

2. From 650 B.C. until 115 B.C. During this era, they gave up the name "Makrib" and assumed the designation of "Kings of Sheba". They also made Ma'rib their capital instead of Sarwah. The ruins of Ma'rib lie at a distance of sixty miles east of San'a.

3. From 115 B.C. until 300 A.D. During this period, the tribe of Himyar conquered the kingdom of Sheba and took Redan for capital instead of Ma'rib. Later on, Redan was called "Zifar". Its ruins still lie on Mudawwar Mountain near the town of "Yarim". During this period, they began to decline and fall. Their trade failed to a very great extent, firstly, because of the Nabetean domain over the north of Hijaz; secondly, because of the Roman superiority over the naval trade routes after the Roman conquest of Egypt, Syria and the north of Hijaz; and thirdly, because of the inter-tribal warfare. Thanks to the three above-mentioned factors, families of Qahtan were disunited and scatteredout.

4. From 300 A.D. until Islam dawned on Yemen. This period witnessed a lot of disorder and turmoil. The great many and civil wars rendered the people of Yemen liable to foreign subjection and hence loss of independence. During this era, the Romans conquered 'Adn and even helped the Abyssinians (Ethiopians) to occupy Yemen for the first time in 340 A.D., making use of the constant intra-tribal conflict of Hamdan and Himyar.

The Abyssinian (Ethiopian) occupation of Yemen lasted until 378 A.D., whereafter Yemen regained its independence. Later on, cracks began to show in Ma'rib Dam which led to the Great Flood (450 or 451 A.D.) mentioned in the Noble Qur'ân. This was a great event which caused the fall of the entire Yemeni civilization and the dispersal of the nations living therein. In 523, Dhu Nawas, a Jew, despatched a great campaign against the Christians of Najran in order to force them to convert into Judaism. Having refused to do so, they were thrown alive into a big ditch where a great fire had been set. The Qur'ân referred to this event: "Cursed were the people of the ditch." [85:4]

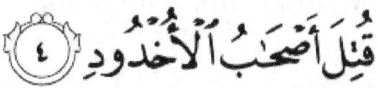

This aroused great wrath among the Christians, and especially the Roman emperors, who not only instigated the Abyssinians (Ethiopians) against Arabs but also assembled a large fleet which helped the Abyssinian (Ethiopian) army, of seventy thousand warriors, to effect a second conquest of Yemen in 525 A.D., under the leadership of Eriat, who was granted rulership over Yemen, a position he held until he was assassinated by one of his army leaders, Abraha, who, after reconciliation with the king of Abyssinia, took rulership over Yemen and, later on, deployed his soldiers to demolish Al-Ka'bah, and, hence, he and his soldiers came to be known as the "Men of the Elephant".

After the "Elephant" incident, the people of Yemen, under the leadership of Ma'dikarib bin Saif Dhu Yazin Al-Himyari, and through Persian assistance, revolted against the Abyssinian (Ethiopian) invaders, restored independence and appointed Ma'dikarib as their king. However, Ma'dikarib was assassinated by an Abyssinian (Ethiopian) he used to have him around for service and protection. The family of Dhu Yazin was thus deprived of royalty forever. Kisra, the Persian king, appointed a Persian ruler over San'a and thus made Yemen a Persian colony. Persian rulers maintained rulership of Yemen until Badhan, the last of them, embraced Islam in 638 A.D., thus terminating the Persian domain over Yemen.

RULERSHIP IN HEERAH:

Ever since Korosh the Great (557-529 B.C.) united the Persians, they ruled Iraq and its neighbourhood. Nobody could shake off their authority until Alexander the Great vanquished their king Dara I and thus subdued the Persians in 326 B.C. Persian lands were thenceforth divided and ruled by kings known as "the Kings of Sects", an era which lasted until 230 A.D. Meanwhile, the Qahtanians occupied some Iraqi territories, and were later followed by some 'Adnanians who managed to share some parts of Mesopotamia with them.

The Persians, under the leadership of Ardashir, who had established the Sasanian state in 226 A.D, regained enough unity and power to subdue the Arabs living in the vicinity of their kingdom, and force Quda'a to leave for Syria, leaving the people of Heerah and Anbar under the Persian domain.

During the time of Ardashir, Juzaima Alwaddah exercised rulership over Heerah, Rabi'a and Mudar, and Mesopotamia. Ardashir had reckoned that it was impossible for him to rule the Arabs directly and prevent them from attacking his borders unless he appointed as king one of them who enjoyed support and power of his tribe. He had also seen that he could make use of them against the Byzantine kings who always used to harass him. At the same time, the Arabs of Iraq could face the Arabs of Syria who were in the hold of Byzantine kings. However, he deemed it fit to keep a Persian battalion under command of the king of Heerah to be used against those Arabs who might rebel against him.

After the death of Juzaima around 268 A.D., 'Amr bin 'Adi bin Nasr Al-Lakhmi was appointed as king by the Persian King Sabour bin Ardashir. 'Amr was the first of the Lakhmi kings who ruled Heerah until the Persians appointed Qabaz bin Fairuz in whose reign appeared someone called Mazdak, who called for dissoluteness in social life. Qabaz, and many of his subjects, embraced Mazdak's religion and even called upon the king of Heerah, Al-Munzir bin Ma' As-Sama', to follow after.

When the latter, because of his pride and self-respect, rejected their orders, Qabaz discharged him and nominated Harith bin 'Amr bin Hajar Al-Kindi, who had accepted the Mazdaki doctrine. No sooner did Kisra Anu Shairwan succeed Qabaz than he, due to hatred of Mazdak's philosophy, killed Mazdak and many of his followers, restored Munzir to the throne of Heerah and gave orders to summon under arrest Harith who sought refuge with Al-Kalb tribe where he spent the rest of his life. Sons of Al-Munzir bin Ma' As-Sama' maintained kingship a long time until An-Nu'man bin Al-Munzir took over. Because of a calumny borne by Zaid bin 'Adi Al-'Abbadi, the Persian king got angry with An- Nu'man and summoned him to his palace. An-Nu'man went secretly to Hani bin Mas'ud, chief of Shaiban tribe, and left his wealth and family under the latter's protection, and then presented himself before the Persian king, who immediately threw him into prison where he perished. Kisra, then, appointed Eyas bin Qubaisa At-Ta'i as king of Heerah. Eyas was ordered to tell Hani bin Mas'ud to deliver An-Nu'man's charge up to Kisra. No sooner than had the Persian king received the fanatically motivated rejection on the part of the Arab chief, he declared war against the tribe of Shaiban and mobilized his troops and warriors under the leadership of King Eyas to a place called Dhee Qar which witnessed a most furious battle wherein the Persians were severely routed by the Arabs for the first time in history. That was very soon after the birth of Prophet Muhammad, peace be upon him, eight months after Eyas bin Qubaisah's rise to power over Heerah. After Eyas, a Persian ruler was appointed over Heerah, but in 632 A.D. the authority there returned to the family of Lukhm when Al-Munzir Al-Ma'rur took over. Hardly had the latter's reign lasted for eight months when Khalid bin Al-Waleed fell upon him with Muslim soldiers.

RULERSHIP IN GEOGRAPHICAL SYRIA:

In the process of the tribal emigrations, some septs of Quda'a reached the borders of Syria where they settled down. They belonged to the family of Sulaih bin Halwan, of whose offspring were the sons of Duj'am bin Sulaih known as Ad-Duja'ima. Such septs of Quda'a were used by the Byzantines in the defence of the Byzantine borders against both Arab Bedouin raiders and the Persians, and enjoyed autonomy for a considerable phase of time which is said to have lasted for the whole second century A.D. One of their most famous kings was Zyiad bin Al-Habula.

Their authority however came to an end upon defeat by the Ghassanides who were consequently granted the proxy rulership over the Arabs of Syria and had Dumat Al-Jandal as their headquarters, which lasted until the battle of Yarmuk in the year 13 A.H. Their last king Jabala bin Al-Aihum embraced Islam during the reign of the Chief of Believers, 'Umar bin Al-Khattab (May Allah be pleased with him).

RULERSHIP IN HIJAZ:

Ishmael (Peace be upon him) administered authority over Makkah as well as custodianship of the Holy Sanctuary throughout his lifetime. Upon his death, at the age of 137, two of his sons, Nabet and Qidar, succeeded him. Later on, their maternal grandfather, Mudad bin 'Amr Al-Jurhumi took over, thus transferring rulership over Makkah to the tribe of Jurhum, preserving a venerable position, though very little authority for Ishmael's sons due to their father's exploits in building the Holy Sanctuary, a position they held until the decline of the tribe of Jurhum shortly before the rise of Bukhtanassar. The political role of the 'Adnanides had begun to gain firmer grounds in Makkah, which could be clearly attested by the fact that upon Bukhtanassar's first invasion of the Arabs in 'Dhati 'Irq', the leader of the Arabs was not from Jurhum.

Upon Bukhtanassar's second invasion in 587 B.C., however, the 'Adnanides were frightened out to Yemen, while Burmia An-Nabi fled to Syria with Ma'ad, but when Bukhtanassar's pressure lessened, Ma'ad returned to Makkah to find none of the tribe of Jurhum except Jursham bin Jalhamah, whose daughter, Mu'ana, was given to Ma'ad as wife who, later, had a son by him named Nizar. On account of difficult living conditions and destitution prevalent in Makkah, the tribe of Jurhum began to ill-treat visitors of the Holy Sanctuary and extort its funds, which aroused resentment and hatred of the 'Adnanides (sons of Bakr bin 'Abd Munaf bin Kinana) who, with the help of the tribe of Khuza'a that had come to settle in a neighbouring area called Marr Az-Zahran, invaded Jurhum and frightened them out of Makkah leaving rulership to Quda'a in the middle of the second century A.D.

Upon leaving Makkah, Jurhum filled up the well of Zamzam, levelled its place and buried a great many things in it. 'Amr bin Al-Harith bin Mudad Al-Jurhumi was reported by Ibn Ishaq, the well-known historian, to have buried the two gold deer together with the Black Stone as well as a lot of jewelry and swords in Zamzam, prior to their sorrowful escape to Yemen. Ishmael's epoch is estimated to have lasted for twenty centuries B.C., which means that Jurhum stayed in Makkah for twenty-one centuries and held rulership there for about twenty centuries. Upon defeat of Jurhum, the tribe of Khuza'a monopolized rulership over Makkah. Mudar tribes, however, enjoyed three privileges:

• The First: Leading pilgrims from 'Arafat to Muzdalifah and then from Mina to the 'Aqabah Stoning Pillar. This was the authority of the family of Al-Ghawth bin Murra, one of the septs of Elias bin Mudar, who were called 'Sofa'. This privilege meant that the pilgrims were not allowed to throw stones at Al-'Aqabah until one of the 'Sofa' men did that. When they had finished stoning and wanted to leave the valley of Mina, 'Sofa' men stood on the two sides of Al-'Aqabah and nobody would pass that position until the men of 'Sofa' passed and cleared the way for the pilgrims. When Sofa perished, the family of Sa'd bin Zaid Manat from Tamim tribe took over.

The Second: Al-Ifadah (leaving for Mina after Muzdalifah) on sacrifice morning, and this was the responsibility of the family of Adwan.

The Third: Deferment of the sacred months, and this was the responsibility of the family of Tamim bin 'Adi from Bani Kinana.

Khuza'a's reign in Makkah lasted for three hundred years, during which, the 'Adnanides spread all over Najd and the sides of Bahrain and Iraq, while small septs of Quraish remained on the sides of Makkah; they were Haloul, Harum and some families of Kinana. They enjoyed no privileges in Makkah or in the Sacred House until the appearance of Qusai bin Kilab, whose father is said to have died when he was still a baby, and whose mother was subsequently married to Rabi'a bin Haram, from the tribe of Bani 'Udhra.

Rabi'a took his wife and her baby to his homeland on the borders of Syria. When Qusai became a young man, he returned to Makkah, which was ruled by Halil bin Habsha from Khuza'a, who gave Qusai his daughter, Hobba, as wife. After Halil's death, a war between Khuza'a and Quraish broke out and resulted in Qusai's taking hold of Makkah and the Sacred House.

THE REASONS OF THIS WAR HAVE BEEN ILLUSTRATED IN THREE VERSIONS:

The First: Having noticed the spread of his offspring, increase of his property and exalt of his honour after Halil's death, Qusai found himself more entitled to shoulder responsibility of rulership over Makkah and custodianship of the Sacred House than the tribes of Khuza'a and Bani Bakr. He also advocated that Quraish were the chiefs of Ishmael's descendants. Therefore he consulted some men from Quraish and Kinana concerning his desire to evacuate Khuza'a and Bani Bakr from Makkah. They took a liking to his opinion and supported him.

The Second: Khuza'a claimed that Halil requested Qusai to hold custodianship of Al-Ka'bah and rulership over Makkah after his death.

The Third: Halil gave the right of Al-Ka'bah service to his daughter Hobba and appointed Abu Ghabshan Al-Khuza'i to function as her agent whereof. Upon Halil's death, Qusai bought this right for a leather bag of wine, which aroused dissatisfaction among the men of Khuza'a and they tried to keep the custodianship of the Sacred House away from Qusai. The latter, however, with the help of Quraish and Kinana, managed to take over and even to expel Khuza'a completely from Makkah. Whatever the truth might have been, the whole affair resulted in the deprivation of Sofa of their privileges, previously mentioned, evacuation of Khuza'a and Bakr from Makkah and transfer of rulership over Makkah and custodianship of the Holy Sanctuary to Qusai, after fierce wars between Qusai and Khuza'a inflicting heavy casualties on both sides, reconciliation and then arbitration of Ya'mur bin 'Awf, from the tribe of Bakr, whose judgement entailed eligibility of Qusai's rulership over

Makkah and custodianship of the Sacred House, Qusai's irresponsibility for Khuza'a's bloodshed, and imposition of blood money on Khuza'a. Qusai's reign over Makkah and the Sacred House began in 440 A.D. and allowed him, and Quraish afterwards, absolute rulership over Makkah and undisputed custodianship of the Sacred House to which Arabs from all over Arabia came to pay homage.

A significant achievement credited to Qusai was the establishment of An-Nadwa House (an assembly house) on the northern side of Al-Ka'bah Mosque, to serve as a meeting place for Quraish. This very house had benefited Quraish a lot because it secured unity of opinions amongst them and cordial solution to their problem.

QUSAI HOWEVER ENJOYED THE FOLLONG PRIVILEGED OF LEADERSHIP AND HONOUR:

1. Presiding over An-Nadwa House meetings where consultations relating to serious issues were conducted, and marriage contracts were announced.

2. The Standard: He monopolized in his hand issues relevant to war launching.

3. Doorkeeping of Al-Ka'bah: He was the only one eligible to open its gate, and was responsible for its service and protection.

4. Providing water for the Pilgrims: This means that he used to fill basins sweetened by dates and raisins for the pilgrims to drink.

5. Feeding Pilgrims: This means making food for pilgrims who could not afford it. Qusai even imposed on Quraish annual land tax, paid at the season of pilgrimage, for food. It is noteworthy however that Qusai singled out 'Abd Manaf, a son of his, for honour and prestige though he was not his elder son ('Abd Ad-Dar was), and entrusted him with such responsibilities as chairing of An-Nadwa House, the standard, the doorkeeping of Al-Ka'bah, providing water and food for pilgrims.

Due to the fact that Qusai's deeds were regarded as unquestionable and his orders inviolable, his death gave no rise to conflicts among his sons, but it later did among his grandchildren, for no sooner than 'Abd Munaf had died, his sons began to have rows with their cousins —sons of 'Abd Ad- Dar, which would have given rise to dissension and fighting among the whole tribe of Quraish, had it not been for a peace treaty whereby posts were reallocated so as to preserve feeding and providing water for pilgrims for the sons of 'Abd Munaf; while An-Nadwa House, the flag and the doorkeeping of Al-Ka'bah were maintained for the sons of 'Abd Ad-Dar. The sons of 'Abd Munaf, however, cast the lot for their charge, and consequently left the charge of food and water giving to Hashim bin 'Abd Munaf, upon whose death, the charge was taken over by a brother of his called Al-Muttalib bin 'Abd Manaf and afterwards by 'Abd Al-Muttalib bin Hashim, the Prophet's grandfather, whose sons assumed this position until the rise of Islam, during which 'Abbas bin 'Abdul-Muttalib was in charge.

Many other posts were distri among people of Quraish for establishing the pillars of a new democratic petite state with government offices and councils similar to those of today. Enlisted as follows are some of these posts.

1. Casting the lots for the idols was allocated to Bani Jumah.

2. Noting of offers and sacrifices, settlement of disputes and relevant issues were to lie in the hands of Bani Sahm.

3. Consultation was to go to Bani Asad.

4. Organization of blood-money and fines was with Bani Tayim.

5. Bearing the national banner was with Bani Omaiyah.

6. The military institute, footmen and cavalry would be Bani Makhzum's responsibility.

7. Bani 'Adi would function as foreign mediators.

RULERSHIP IN PAN-ARABIA:

We have previously mentioned the Qahtanide and 'Adnanide emigrations, and division of Arabia between these two tribes. Those tribes dwelling near Heerah were subordinate to the Arabian king of Heerah, while those dwelling in the Syrian semi-desert were under domain of the Arabian Ghassanide king, a sort of dependency that was in reality formal rather than actual. However, those living in the hinder deserts enjoyed full autonomy.

Heads of tribes enjoyed dictatorial privileges similar to those of kings, and were rendered full obedience and subordination in both war and peace. Rivalry among cousins for rulership, however, often drove them to outdo one another in entertaining guests, affecting generosity, wisdom and chivalry for the sole purpose of outranking their rivals, and gaining fame among people especially poets who were the official spokesmen at the time. Heads of tribes and masters had special claims to spoils of war such as the quarter of the spoils, whatever he chose for himself, or found on his way back or even the remaining indivisible spoils.

THE POLITICAL SITUATION:

The three Arab regions adjacent to foreigners suffered great weakness and inferiority. The people there were either masters or slaves, rulers or subordinates. Masters, especially the foreigners, had claim to every advantage; slaves had nothing but responsibilities to shoulder. In other words, arbitrary autocratic rulership brought about encroachment on the rights of subordinates, ignorance, oppression, iniquity, injustice and hardship, and turning them into people groping in darkness and ignorance, viz., fertile land which rendered its fruits to the rulers and men of power to extravagantly dissipate on their pleasures and enjoyments, whims and desires, tyranny and aggression. The tribes living near these regions were fluctuating between Syria and Iraq, whereas those living inside Arabia were disunited and governed by tribal conflicts and racial and religious disputes.

They had neither a king to sustain their independence nor a supporter to seek advice from, or depend upon, in hardships. The rulers of Hijaz, however, were greatly esteemed and respected by the Arabs, and were considered as rulers and servants of the religious center. Rulership of Hijaz was, in fact, a mixture of secular and official precedence as well as religious leadership. They ruled among the Arabs in the name of religious leadership and always monopolized the custodianship of the Holy Sanctuary and its neighbourhood. They looked after the interests of Al-Ka'bah visitors and were in charge of putting Abraham's code into effect. They even had such offices and departments like those of the parliaments of today. However, they were too weak to carry the heavy burden, as this evidently came to light during the Abyssinian (Ethiopian) invasion.

RELIGIONS OF THE ARABS

Most of the Arabs had complied with the call of Ishmael (Peace be upon him) , and professed the religion of his father Abraham (Peace be upon him) They had worshipped Allâh, professed His Oneness and followed His religion a long time until they forgot part of what they had been reminded of. However, they still maintained such fundamental beliefs such as monotheism as well as various other aspects of Abraham's religion, until the time when a chief of Khuza'a, namely 'Amr bin Luhai, who was renowned for righteousness, charity, reverence and care for religion, and was granted unreserved love and obedience by his tribesmen, came back from a trip to Syria where he saw people worship idols, a phenomenon he approved of and believed it to be righteous since Syria was the locus of Messengers and Scriptures, he brought with him an idol (Hubal) which he placed in the middle of Al-Ka'bah and summoned people to worship it. Readily enough, paganism spread all over Makkah and, thence, to Hijaz, people of Makkah being custodians of not only the Sacred House but the whole Haram as well. A great many idols, bearing different names, were introduced into the area.

An idol called 'Manat', for instance, was worshipped in a place known as Al-Mushallal near Qadid on the Red Sea. Another, 'Al-Lat' in Ta'if, a third, 'Al-'Uzza' in the valley of Nakhlah, and so on and so forth. Polytheism prevailed and the number of idols increased everywhere in Hijaz. It was even mentioned that 'Amr bin Luhai, with the help of a jinn companion who told him that the idols of Noah's folk – Wadd, Suwa', Yaguth, Ya'uk and Nasr – were buried in Jeddah, dug them out and took them to Tihama. Upon pilgrimage time, the idols were distributed among the tribes to take back home. Every tribe, and house, had their own idols, and the Sacred House was also overcrowded with them. On the Prophet's conquest of Makkah, 360 idols were found around Al-Ka'bah. He broke them down and had them removed and burned up. Polytheism and worship of idols became the most prominent feature of the religion of pre-Islam Arabs despite alleged profession of Abraham's religion.

Traditions and ceremonies of the worship of their idols had been mostly created by 'Amr bin Luhai, and were deemed as good innovations rather than deviations from Abraham's religion. Some features of their worship of idols were:

• Self-devotion to the idols, seeking refuge with them, acclamation of their names, calling for their help in hardship, and supplication to them for fulfillment of wishes, hopefully that the idols (i.e., heathen gods) would mediate with Allâh for the fulfillment of people's wishes.

• Performing pilgrimage to the idols, circumrotation round them, self-abasement and even prostrating themselves before them.

• Seeking favour of idols through various kinds of sacrifices and immolations, which is mentioned in the Qur'ânic verses:

• "And that which is sacrificed (slaughtered) on An-Nusub (stone-altars)" [5:3]

حُرِّمَتْ عَلَيْكُمُ ٱلْمَيْتَةُ وَٱلدَّمُ وَلَحْمُ ٱلْخِنزِيرِ وَمَآ أُهِلَّ لِغَيْرِ ٱللَّهِ بِهِۦ وَٱلْمُنْخَنِقَةُ وَٱلْمَوْقُوذَةُ وَٱلْمُتَرَدِّيَةُ وَٱلنَّطِيحَةُ وَمَآ أَكَلَ ٱلسَّبُعُ إِلَّا مَا ذَكَّيْتُمْ وَمَا ذُبِحَ عَلَى ٱلنُّصُبِ وَأَن تَسْتَقْسِمُوا۟ بِٱلْأَزْلَـٰمِ ذَٰلِكُمْ فِسْقٌ ٱلْيَوْمَ يَئِسَ ٱلَّذِينَ كَفَرُوا۟ مِن دِينِكُمْ فَلَا تَخْشَوْهُمْ وَٱخْشَوْنِ ٱلْيَوْمَ أَكْمَلْتُ لَكُمْ دِينَكُمْ وَأَتْمَمْتُ عَلَيْكُمْ نِعْمَتِى وَرَضِيتُ لَكُمُ ٱلْإِسْلَـٰمَ دِينًا فَمَنِ ٱضْطُرَّ فِى مَخْمَصَةٍ غَيْرَ مُتَجَانِفٍ لِّإِثْمٍ فَإِنَّ ٱللَّهَ غَفُورٌ رَّحِيمٌ ۝٣

Allâh also says:

• "Eat not (O believers) of that (meat) on which Allâh's Name has not been pronounced (at the time of the slaughtering of the animal)." [6:121]

وَلَا تَأْكُلُوا۟ مِمَّا لَمْ يُذْكَرِ ٱسْمُ ٱللَّهِ عَلَيْهِ وَإِنَّهُۥ لَفِسْقٌ ۗ وَإِنَّ ٱلشَّيَٰطِينَ لَيُوحُونَ إِلَىٰٓ أَوْلِيَآئِهِمْ لِيُجَٰدِلُوكُمْ ۖ وَإِنْ أَطَعْتُمُوهُمْ إِنَّكُمْ لَمُشْرِكُونَ ﴿١٢١﴾

• Consecration of certain portions of food, drink, cattle, and crops to idols. Surprisingly enough, portions were also consecrated to Allâh Himself, but people often found reasons to transfer parts of Allâh's portion to idols, but never did the opposite. To this effect, the Qur'ânic verses go:

• "And they assign to Allâh a share of the tilth and cattle which He has created, and they say: 'This is for Allâh according to their pretending, and this is for our (Allâh's so-called) partners.' But the share of their (Allâh's so-called) 'partners', reaches not Allâh, while the share of Allâh reaches their (Allâh's so-called) 'partners'. Evil is the way they judge." [6:136]

وَجَعَلُوا۟ لِلَّهِ مِمَّا ذَرَأَ مِنَ ٱلْحَرْثِ وَٱلْأَنْعَٰمِ نَصِيبًا فَقَالُوا۟ هَٰذَا لِلَّهِ بِزَعْمِهِمْ وَهَٰذَا لِشُرَكَآئِنَا ۖ فَمَا كَانَ لِشُرَكَآئِهِمْ فَلَا يَصِلُ إِلَى ٱللَّهِ ۖ وَمَا كَانَ لِلَّهِ فَهُوَ يَصِلُ إِلَىٰ شُرَكَآئِهِمْ ۗ سَآءَ مَا يَحْكُمُونَ ﴿١٣٦﴾

• Currying favours with these idols through votive offerings of crops and cattle, to which effect.

• "And according to their pretending, they say that such and such cattle and crops are forbidden, and none should eat of them except those whom we allow. And (they say) there are cattle forbidden to be used for burden or any other work, and cattle on which (at slaughtering) the Name of Allâh is not pronounced; lying against Him (Allâh)." [6:138]

$$\text{وَقَالُوا۟ هَـٰذِهِۦٓ أَنْعَـٰمٌ وَحَرْثٌ حِجْرٌ لَّا يَطْعَمُهَآ إِلَّا مَن نَّشَآءُ بِزَعْمِهِمْ وَأَنْعَـٰمٌ حُرِّمَتْ ظُهُورُهَا وَأَنْعَـٰمٌ لَّا يَذْكُرُونَ ٱسْمَ ٱللَّهِ عَلَيْهَا ٱفْتِرَآءً عَلَيْهِ ۚ سَيَجْزِيهِم بِمَا كَانُوا۟ يَفْتَرُونَ ١٣٨}$$

• Dedication of certain animals (such as Bahira, Sa'iba, Wasila and Hami) to idols, which meant sparing such animals from useful work for the sake of these heathen gods. Bahira, as reported by the well-known historian, Ibn Ish, was daughter of Sa'iba which was a female camel that gave birth to ten successive female animals, but no male ones, was set free and forbidden to yoke, burden or being sheared off its wool, or milked (but for guests to drink from); and so was done to all her female offspring which were given the name 'Bahira', after having their ears slit. The Wasila was a female sheep which had ten successive female daughters in five pregnancies. Any new births from this Wasila were assigned only for male people. The Hami was a male camel which produced ten progressive females, and was thus similarly forbidden. In mention of this, the Qur'ânic verses go:

• "Allâh has not instituted things like Bahira (a she-camel whose milk was spared for the idols and nobody was allowed to milk it) or a Sa'iba (a she camel let loose for free pasture for their false gods, e.g. idols, etc., and nothing was allowed to be carried on it), or a Wasila (a she-camel set free for idols because it has given birth to a she-camel at its first delivery and then again gives birth to a she-camel at its second delivery) or a Hâm (a stallion-camel freed from work for their idols, after it had finished a number of copulations assigned for it, all these animals were liberated in honour of idols as practised by pagan Arabs in the pre-Islamic period). But those who disbelieve, invent lies against Allâh, and most of them have no understanding." [5:103]

مَا جَعَلَ ٱللَّهُ مِنۢ بَحِيرَةٍ وَلَا سَآئِبَةٍ وَلَا وَصِيلَةٍ وَلَا حَامٍ وَلَٰكِنَّ ٱلَّذِينَ كَفَرُواْ يَفْتَرُونَ عَلَى ٱللَّهِ ٱلْكَذِبَ وَأَكْثَرُهُمْ لَا يَعْقِلُونَ ۝

Allâh also says:

• "And they say: What is in the bellies of such and such cattle (milk or foetus) is for our males alone, and forbidden to our females (girls and women), but if it is born dead, then all have shares therein." [6:139]

وَقَالُواْ مَا فِى بُطُونِ هَٰذِهِ ٱلْأَنْعَٰمِ خَالِصَةٌ لِّذُكُورِنَا وَمُحَرَّمٌ عَلَىٰٓ أَزْوَٰجِنَا ۖ وَإِن يَكُن مَّيْتَةً فَهُمْ فِيهِ شُرَكَآءُ ۚ سَيَجْزِيهِمْ وَصْفَهُمْ ۚ إِنَّهُۥ حَكِيمٌ عَلِيمٌ ۝

It has been authentically reported that such superstitions were first invented by 'Amr bin Luhai.

The Arabs believed that such idols, or heathen gods, would bring them nearer to Allâh, lead them to Him, and mediate with Him for their sake, to which effect, the Qur'ân says:

- "We worship them only that they may bring us near to Allâh." [39:3]

$$\text{أَلَا لِلَّهِ الدِّينُ الْخَالِصُ وَالَّذِينَ اتَّخَذُوا مِن دُونِهِ أَوْلِيَاءَ مَا نَعْبُدُهُمْ إِلَّا لِيُقَرِّبُونَا إِلَى اللَّهِ زُلْفَىٰ إِنَّ اللَّهَ يَحْكُمُ بَيْنَهُمْ فِي مَا هُمْ فِيهِ يَخْتَلِفُونَ ۗ إِنَّ اللَّهَ لَا يَهْدِي مَنْ هُوَ كَاذِبٌ كَفَّارٌ ۝٣}$$

"And they worship besides Allâh things that hurt them not, nor profit them, and they say: These are our intercessors with Allâh." [10:18]

$$\text{وَيَعْبُدُونَ مِن دُونِ اللَّهِ مَا لَا يَضُرُّهُمْ وَلَا يَنفَعُهُمْ وَيَقُولُونَ هَٰؤُلَاءِ شُفَعَاؤُنَا عِندَ اللَّهِ ۚ قُلْ أَتُنَبِّئُونَ اللَّهَ بِمَا لَا يَعْلَمُ فِي السَّمَاوَاتِ وَلَا فِي الْأَرْضِ ۚ سُبْحَانَهُ وَتَعَالَىٰ عَمَّا يُشْرِكُونَ ۝١٨}$$

Another divinatory tradition among the Arabs was casting of Azlam (i.e. featherless arrows which were of three kinds: one showing 'yes', another 'no' and a third was blank) which they used to do in case of serious matters like travel, marriage and the like. If the lot showed 'yes', they would do, if 'no', they would delay for the next year. Other kinds of Azlam were cast for water, blood-money or showed 'from you', 'not from you', or 'Mulsaq' (consociated). In cases of doubt in filiation they would resort to the idol of Hubal, with a hundred-camel gift, for the arrow caster. Only the arrows would then decide the sort of relationship. If the arrow showed (from you), then it was decided that the child belonged to the tribe; if it showed (from others), he would then be regarded as an ally, but if (consociated) appeared, the person would retain his position but with no lineage or alliance contract.

This was very much like gambling and arrow-shafting whereby they used to divide the meat of the camels they slaughtered according to this tradition. Moreover, they used to have a deep conviction in the tidings of soothsayers, diviners and astrologers. A soothsayer used to traffic in the business of foretelling future events and claim knowledge of private secrets and having jinn subordinates who would communicate the news to him. Some soothsayers claimed that they could uncover the unknown by means of a granted power, while other diviners boasted they could divulge the secrets through a cause-and-effect-inductive process that would lead to detecting a stolen commodity, location of a theft, a stray animal, and the like. The astrologer belonged to a third category who used to observe the stars and calculate their movements and orbits whereby he would foretell the future. Lending credence to this news constituted a clue to their conviction that attached special significance to the movements of particular stars with regard to rainfall.

The belief in signs as betokening future events, was, of course common among the Arabians. Some days and months and particular animals were regarded as ominous. They also believed that the soul of a murdered person would fly in the wilderness and would never rest at rest until revenge was taken. Superstition was rampant. Should a deer or bird, when released, turn right then what they embarked on would be regarded auspicious, otherwise they would get pessimistic and withhold from pursuing it.

People of pre-Islamic period, whilst believing in superstition, they still retained some of the Abrahamic traditions such as devotion to the Holy Sanctuary, circumambulation, observance of pilgrimage, the vigil on 'Arafah and offering sacrifices, all of these were observed fully despite some innovations that adulterated these holy rituals. Quraish, for example, out of arrogance, feeling of superiority to other tribes and pride in their custodianship of the Sacred House, would refrain from going to 'Arafah with the crowd, instead they would stop short at Muzdalifah. The Noble Qur'ân rebuked and told them:

- "Then depart from the place whence all the people depart." [2:199]

ثُمَّ أَفِيضُوا۟ مِنْ حَيْثُ أَفَاضَ ٱلنَّاسُ وَٱسْتَغْفِرُوا۟ ٱللَّهَ ۚ إِنَّ ٱللَّهَ غَفُورٌ رَّحِيمٌ ﴿١٩٩﴾

Another heresy, deeply established in their social tradition, dictated that they would not eat dried yoghurt or cooked fat, nor would they enter a tent made of camel hair or seek shade unless in a house of adobe bricks, so long as they were committed to the intention of pilgrimage. They also, out of a deeply-rooted misconception, denied pilgrims, other than Makkans, access to the food they had brought when they wanted to make pilgrimage or lesser pilgrimage. They ordered pilgrims coming from outside Makkah to circumambulate Al-Ka'bah in Quraish uniform clothes, but if they could not afford them, men were to do so in a state of nudity, and women with only some piece of cloth to hide their groins. Allâh says in this concern:

- "O Children of Adam! Take your adornment (by wearing your clean clothes), while praying [and going round (the Tawaf of) the Ka'bah". [7:31]

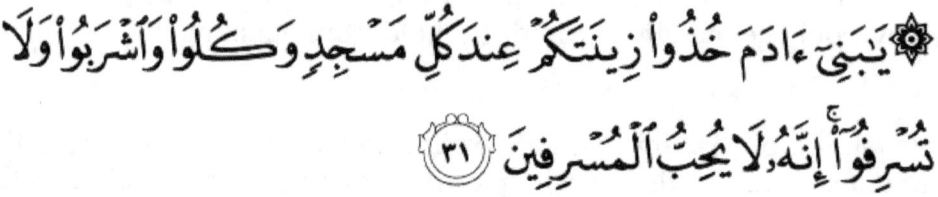

If men or women were generous enough to go round Al-Ka'bah in their clothes, they had to discard them after circumambulation for good. When the Makkans were in a pilgrimage consecration state, they would not enter their houses through the doors but through holes they used to dig in the back walls. They used to regard such behaviour as deeds of piety and god-fearing. This practice was prohibited by the Qur'ân:

• "It is not Al-Birr (piety, righteousness, etc.) that you enter the houses from the back but Al-Birr (is the quality of the one) who fears Allâh. So enter houses through their proper doors, and fear Allâh that you may be successful." [2:189]

﷽ يَسْـَٔلُونَكَ عَنِ ٱلْأَهِلَّةِ قُلْ هِىَ مَوَٰقِيتُ لِلنَّاسِ وَٱلْحَجِّ وَلَيْسَ ٱلْبِرُّ بِأَن تَأْتُواْ ٱلْبُيُوتَ مِن ظُهُورِهَا وَلَـٰكِنَّ ٱلْبِرَّ مَنِ ٱتَّقَىٰ وَأْتُواْ ٱلْبُيُوتَ مِنْ أَبْوَٰبِهَا وَٱتَّقُواْ ٱللَّهَ لَعَلَّكُمْ تُفْلِحُونَ ۝١٨٩

Such was the religious life in Arabia, polytheism, idolatry, and superstition. Judaism, Christianity, Magianism and Sabianism, however, could find their ways easily into Arabia. The migration of the Jews from Palestine to Arabia passed through two phases: first, as a result of the pressure to which they were exposed, the destruction of their temple, and taking most of them as captives to Babylon, at the hand of the King Bukhtanassar. In the year B.C. 587 some Jews left Palestine for Hijaz and settled in the northern areas whereof. The second phase started with the Roman occupation of Palestine under the leadership of Roman Buts in 70 A.D. This resulted in a tidal wave of Jewish migration into Hijaz, and Yathrib, Khaibar and Taima', in particular.

Here, they made proselytes of several tribes, built forts and castles, and lived in villages. Judaism managed to play an important role in the pre-Islam political life. When Islam dawned on that land, there had already been several famous Jewish tribes — Khabeer, Al-Mustaliq, An-Nadeer, Quraizah and Qainuqa'. In some versions, the Jewish tribes counted as many as twenty.

Judaism was introduced into Yemen by someone called As'ad Abi Karb. He had gone to fight in Yathrib and there he embraced Judaism and then went back taking with him two rabbis from Bani Quraizah to instruct thpeople of Yemen in this new religion. Judaism found a fertile soil there to propagate and gain adherents. After his death, his son Yusuf Dhu Nawas rose to power, attacked the Christian community in Najran and ordered them to embrace Judaism. When they refused, he ordered that a pit of fire be dug and all the Christians indiscriminately be dropped to burn therein. Estimates say that between 20- 40 thousand Christians were killed in that human massacre. The Qur'ân related part of that story in Al- Buruj (zodiacal signs) Chapter.

Christianity had first made its appearance in Arabia following the entry of the Abyssinian (Ethiopian) and Roman colonists into that country. The Abyssinian (Ethiopian) colonization forces in league with Christian missions entered Yemen as a retaliatory reaction for the iniquities of Dhu Nawas, and started vehemently to propagate their faith ardently. They even built a church and called it Yemeni Al-Ka'bah with the aim of directing the Arab pilgrimage caravans towards Yemen, and then made an attempt to demolish the Sacred House in Makkah. Allâh, the Almighty, however did punish them and made an example of them – here and hereafter.

A Christian missionary called Fimion, and known for his ascetic behaviour and working miracles, had likewise infiltrated into Najran. There he called people to Christianity, and by virtue of his honesty and truthful devotion, he managed to persuade them to respond positively to his invitation and embrace Christianity.

The principal tribes that embraced Christianity were Ghassan, Taghlib, Tai' and some Himyarite kings as well as other tribes living on the borders of the Roman Empire.

Magianism was also popular among the Arabs living in the neighbourhood of Persia, Iraq, Bahrain, Al- Ahsâ' and some areas on the Arabian Gulf coast.

Some Yemenis are also reported to have professed Magianism during the Persian occupation. As for Sabianism, excavations in Iraq revealed that it had been popular amongst Kaldanian folks, the Syrians and Yemenis. With the advent of Judaism and Christianity, however, Sabianism began to give way to the new religions, although it retained some followers mixed or adjacent to the Magians in Iraq and the Arabian Gulf.

THE RELIGIOUS SITUATION:

Such was the religious life of the Arabians before the advent of Islam. The role that the religions prevalent played was so marginal, in fact it was next to nothing. The polytheists, who faked Abrahamism, were so far detached from its precepts, and totally oblivious of its immanent good manners. They plunged into disobedience and ungodliness, and developed certain peculiar religious superstitions that managed to leave a serious impact on the religious and socio-political life in the whole of Arabia.

Judaism turned into abominable hypocrisy in league with hegemony. Rabbis turned into lords to the exclusion of the Lord. They got involved in the practice of dictatorial subjection of people. Their sole target turned into acquisition of wealth and power even if it were at the risk of losing their religion, or the emergence of atheism and disbelief.

Christianity likewise opened its doors wide to polytheism, and got too difficult to comprehend as a heavenly religion. As a religious practice, it developed a sort of peculiar medley of man and God. It exercised no bearing whatsoever on the souls of the Arabs who professed it simply because it was alien to their style of life and did not have the least relationship with their practical life. People of other religions were similar to the polytheists with respect to their inclinations, dogmas, customs and traditions.

ASPECT OF PRE-ISLAMIC ARABIAN SOCIETY

After the research we have made into the religious and political life of Arabia, it is appropriate to speak briefly about the social, economic and ethical conditions prevalent therein.

SOCIAL LIFE OF THE ARABS:

The Arabian Society presented a social medley, with different and heterogeneous social strata. The status of the woman among the nobility recorded an advanced degree of esteem. The woman enjoyed a considerable portion of free will, and her decision would most often be enforced. She was so highly cherished that blood would be easily shed in defence of her honour. In fact, she was the most decisive key to bloody fight or friendly peace. These privileges notwithstanding, the family system in Arabia was wholly patriarchal. The marriage contract rested completely in the hands of the woman's legal guardian whose words with regard to her marital status could never be questioned.

On the other hand, there were other social strata where prostitution and indecency were rampant and in full operation. Abu Da'ûd, on the authority of 'Aishah (May Allah be pleased with her) reported four kinds of marriage in pre-Islamic Arabia: The first was similar to present-day marriage procedures, in which case a man gives his daughter in marriage to another man after a dowry has been agreed on. In the second, the husband would send his wife – after the menstruation period – to cohabit with another man in order to conceive. After conception her husband would, if he desired, have a sexual intercourse with her. A third kind was that a group of less than ten men would have sexual intercourse with a woman. If she conceived and gave birth to a child, she would send for these men, and nobody could abstain. They would come together to her house. She would say: 'You know what you have done. I have given birth to a child and it is your child' (pointing to one of them). The man meant would have to accept. The fourth kind was that a lot of men would have sexual intercourse with a certain woman (a whore).

She would not prevent anybody. Such women used to put a certain flag at their gates to invite in anyone who liked. If this whore got pregnant and gave birth to a child, she would collect those men, and a seeress would tell whose child it was. The appointed father would take the child and declare him/her his own. When Prophet Muhammad (Peace be upon him) declared Islam in Arabia, he cancelled all these forms of sexual contacts except that of present Islamic marriage

Women always accompanied men in their wars. The winners would freely have sexual intercourse with such women, but disgrace would follow the children conceived in this way all their lives.

Pre-Islam Arabs had no limited number of wives. They could marry two sisters at the same time, or even the wives of their fathers if divorced or widowed. Divorce was to a very great extent in the power of the husband.

The obscenity of adultery prevailed almost among all social classes except few men and women whose self-dignity prevented them from committing such an act. Free women were in much better conditions than the female slaves who constituted the greatest calamity. It seemed that the greatest majority of pre-Islam Arabs did not feel ashamed of committing this obscenity. Abu Da'ûd reported: A man stood up in front of Prophet Muhammad (Peace be upon him) and said: "O Prophet of Allâh! The boy is my son. I had sexual intercourse with his mother in the pre-Islamic period." The Prophet (Peace be upon him) said:

- "No claim in Islam for pre-Islamic affairs. The child is to be attributed to the one on whose bed it was born, and stoning is the lot of a fornicator."

With respect to the pre-Islam Arab's relation with his offspring, we see that life in Arabia was paradoxical and presented a gloomy picture of contrasts.

Whilst some Arabs held children dear to their hearts and cherished them greatly, others buried their female children alive because an illusory fear of poverty and shame weighed heavily on them. The practice of infanticide cannot be seen as irrevocably rampant because of their dire need for male children to guard themselves against their enemies.

Another aspect of the Arabs' life which deserves mention is the bedouin's deep-seated emotional attachment to his clan. Family, or perhaps tribal-pride, was one of the strongest passions with him. The doctrine of unity of blood as the principle that bound the Arabs into a social unity was formed and supported by tribal-pride. Their undisputed motto was: Support your brother whether he is an oppressor or oppressed" in its literal meaning; they disregarded the Islamic amendment which states that supporting an oppressor brother implies deterring him from transgression.

Avarice for leadership, and keen sense of emulation often resulted in bitter tribal warfare despite descendency from one common ancestor. In this regard, the continued bloody conflicts of Aws and Khazraj, 'Abs and Dhubyan, Bakr and Taghlib, etc. are striking examples.

Inter-tribal relationships were fragile and weak due to continual inter-tribal wars of attrition. Deep devotion to religious superstitions and some customs held in veneration, however, used to curb their impetuous tendency to quench their thirst for blood. In other cases, there were the motives of, and respect for, alliance, loyalty and dependency which could successfully bring about a spirit of rapport, and abort groundless bases of dispute. A time-honoured custom of suspending hostilities during the prohibited months (Muharram, Rajab, Dhul-Qa'dah, and Dhul-Hijjah) functioned favourably and provided an opportunity for them to earn their living and coexist in peace. We may sum up the social situation in Arabia by saying that the Arabs of the pre-Islamic period were groping about in the dark and ignorance, entangled in a mesh of superstitions paralyzing their mind and driving them to lead an animal-like life. The woman was a marketable commodity and regarded as a piece of inanimate property.

Inter-tribal relationships were fragile. Avarice for wealth and involvement in futile wars were the main objectives that governed their chiefs' self-centred policies.

THE ECONOMIC SITUATION:

The economic situation ran in line with the social atmosphere. The Arabian ways of living would illustrate this phenomenon quite clearly. Trade was the most common means of providing their needs of life. The trade journeys could not be fulfilled unless security of caravan routes and inter-tribal peaceful co-existence were provided – two imperative exigencies unfortunately lacking in Arabia except during the prohibited months within which the Arabs held their assemblies of 'Ukaz, Dhil-Majaz, Mijannah and others. Industry was alien to the Arabian psychology. Most of available industries of knitting and tannage in Arabia were done by people coming from Yemen, Heerah and the borders of Syria. Inside Arabia there was some sort of farming and stock-breeding. Almost all the Arabian women worked in yarn spinning but even this practice was continually threatened by wars. On the whole, poverty, hunger and insufficient clothing were the prevailing features in Arabia, economically.

ETHICS:

We cannot deny that the pre-Islam Arabs had such a large bulk of evils. Admittedly, vices and evils, utterly rejected by reason, were rampant amongst the pre-Islam Arabs, but this could never screen off the surprise-provoking existence of highly praiseworthy virtues, of which we could adduce the following:

1. Hospitality: They used to emulate one another at hospitality and take utmost pride in it. Almost half of their poetry heritage was dedicated to the merits and nobility attached to entertaining one's guest. They were generous and hospitable on the point of fault.

They would sacrifice their private sustenance to a cold or hungry guest. They would not hesitate to incur heavy blood-money and relevant burdens just to stop blood-shed, and consequently merit praise and eulogy.

2. In the context of hospitality, there springs up their common habits of drinking wine which was regarded as a channel branching out of generosity and showing hospitality. Wine drinking was a genuine source of pride for the Arabs of the pre-Islamic period. The great poets of that era never forgot to include their suspending odes the most ornate lines pregnant with boasting and praise of drinking orgies. Even the word 'grapes' in Arabic is identical to generosity in both pronunciation and spelling. Gambling was also another practice of theirs closely associated with generosity since the proceeds would always go to charity. Even the Noble Qur'ân does not play down the benefits that derive from wine drinking and gambling, but also says, "And the sin of them is greater than their benefit." [2:219]

3. Keeping a covenant: For the Arab, to make a promise was to run into debt. He would never grudge the death of his children or destruction of his household just to uphold the deep-rooted tradition of covenant-keeping. The literature of that period is rich in stories highlighting this merit.

4. Sense of honour and repudiation of injustice: This attribute stemmed mainly from excess courage, keen sense of self-esteem and impetuosity. The Arab was always in revolt against the least allusion to humiliation or slackness. He would never hesitate to sacrifice himself to maintain his ever alert sense of self-respect.

5. Firm will and determination: An Arab would never desist an avenue conducive to an object of pride or a standing of honour, even if it were at the expense of his life.

6. Forbearance, perseverance and mildness: The Arab regarded these traits with great admiration, no wonder, his impetuosity and courage-based life was sadly wanting in them.

7. Pure and simple bedouin life, still untarnished with accessories of deceptive urban appearances, was a driving reason to his nature of truthfulness and honesty, and detachment from intrigue and treachery.

Such priceless ethics coupled with a favourable geographical position of Arabia were in fact the factors that lay behind selecting the Arabs to undertake the burden of communicating the Message (of Islam) and leading mankind down a new course of life. In this regard, these ethics per se, though detrimental in some areas, and in need of rectification in certain aspects, were greatly invaluable to the ultimate welfare of the human community and Islam has did it completely.

The most priceless ethics, next to covenant-keeping, were no doubt their sense of self-esteem and strong determination, two human traits indispensable in combatting evil and eliminating moral corruption on the one hand, and establishing a good and justice-orientated society, on the other. Actually, the life of the Arabs in the pre-Islamic period was rich in other countless virtues we do not need to enumerate for the time being.

THE LINEAGE AND THE FAMILY OF MUHAMMAD
(Peace be upon him)

With respect to the lineage of Prophet Muhammad (Peace be upon him), there are three versions: The first was authenticated by biographers and genealogists and states that Muhammad's genealogy has been traced to 'Adnan. The second is subject to controversies and doubt, and traces his lineage beyond 'Adnan back to Abraham. The third version, with some parts definitely incorrect, traces his lineage beyond Abraham back to Adam (Peace be upon him) after this rapid review, now ample details are believed to be necessary.

The first part: Muhammad bin 'Abdullah bin 'Abdul-Muttalib (who was called Shaiba) bin Hashim, (named 'Amr) bin 'Abd Munaf (called Al-Mugheera) bin Qusai (also called Zaid) bin Kilab bin Murra bin Ka'b bin Lo'i bin Ghalib bin Fahr (who was called Quraish and whose tribe was called after him) bin Malik bin An-Nadr (so called Qais) bin Kinana bin Khuzaiman bin Mudrikah (who was called 'Amir) bin Elias bin Mudar bin Nizar bin Ma'ad bin 'Adnan.

The second part: 'Adnan bin Add bin Humaisi' bin Salaman bin Aws bin Buz bin Qamwal bin Obai bin 'Awwam bin Nashid bin Haza bin Bildas bin Yadlaf bin Tabikh bin Jahim bin Nahish bin Makhi bin Aid bin 'Abqar bin 'Ubaid bin Ad-Da'a bin Hamdan bin Sanbir bin Yathrabi bin Yahzin bin Yalhan bin Ar'awi bin Aid bin Deshan bin Aisar bin Afnad bin Aiham bin Muksar bin Nahith bin Zarih bin Sami bin Mazzi bin 'Awda bin Aram bin Qaidar bin Ishmael son of Abraham (Peace be upon them).

The third part: beyond Abraham (Peace be upon him), Ibn Tarih (Azar) bin Nahur bin Saru' bin Ra'u bin Falikh bin Abir bin Shalikh bin Arfakhshad bin Sam bin Noah (Peace be upon him), bin Lamik bin Mutwashlack bin Akhnukh [who was said to be Prophet Idris (Enoch) (Peace be upon him)bin Yarid bin Mahla'il bin Qabin Anusha bin Shith bin Adam (Peace be upon him)

THE PROPHETIC FAMILY:

The family of Prophet Muhammad (Peace be upon him) is called the Hashimite family after his grandfather Hashim bin 'Abd Munaf. Let us now speak a little about Hashim and his descendants:

1. Hashim: As we have previously mentioned, he was the one responsible for giving food and water to the pilgrims. This had been his charge when the sons of 'Abd Munaf and those of 'Abd Ad-Dar compromised on dividing the charges between them. Hashim was wealthy and honest.

He was the first to offer the pilgrims sopped bread in broth. His first name was 'Amr but he was called Hashim because he had been in the practice of crumbling bread (for the pilgrims). He was also the first man who started Quraish's two journeys of summer and winter. It was reported that he went to Syria as a merchant. In Madinah, he married Salma — the daughter of 'Amr from Bani 'Adi bin An-Najjar. He spent some time with her in Madinah then he left for Syria again while she was pregnant. He died in Ghazza in Palestine in 497 A.D. Later, his wife gave birth to 'Abdul-Muttalib and named him Shaiba for the white hair in his head, and brought him up in her father's house in Madinah. None of his family in Makkah learned of his birth. Hashim had four sons; Asad, Abu Saifi, Nadla and 'Abdul-Muttalib, and five daughters Ash-Shifa, Khalida, Da'ifa, Ruqyah and Jannah.

2. 'Abdul-Muttalib: We have already known that after the death of Hashim, the charge of pilgrims' food and water went to his brother Al-Muttalib bin 'Abd Munaf (who was honest, generous and trustworthy). When 'Abdul-Muttalib reached the age of boyhood, his uncle Al-Muttalib heard of him and went to Madinah to fetch him. When he saw him, tears filled his eyes and rolled down his cheeks, he embraced him and took him on his camel. The boy, however abstained from going with him to Makkah until he took his mother's consent. Al-Muttalib asked her to send the boy with him to Makkah, but she refused. He managed to convince her saying: "Your son is going to Makkah to restore his father's authority, and to live in the vicinity of the Sacred House." There in Makkah, people wondered at seeing Abdul-Muttalib, and they considered him the slave of Muttalib. Al-Muttalib said: "He is my nephew, the son of my brother Hashim." The boy was brought up in Al-Muttalib's house, but later on Al-Muttalib died in Bardman in Yemen so 'Abdul- Muttalib took over and managed to maintain his people's prestige and outdo his grandfathers in his honourable behaviour which gained him Makkah's deep love and high esteem.

3. When Al-Muttalib died, Nawfal usurped 'Abdul-Muttalib of his charges, so the latter asked for help from Quraish but they abstained from extending any sort of support to either of them. Consequently, he wrote to his uncles of Bani An-Najjar (his mother's brothers) to come to his aid. His uncle, Abu Sa'd bin 'Adi (his mother's brother) marched to Makkah at the head of eighty horsemen and camped in Abtah in Makkah.

'Abdul-Muttalib received the men and invited them to go to his house but Abu Sa'd said: "Not before I meet Nawfal." He found Nawfal sitting with some old men of Quraish in the shade of Al-Ka'bah. Abu Sa'd drew his sword and said: "I swear by Allâh that if you don't restore to my nephew what you have taken, I will kill you with this sword." Nawfal was thus forced to give up what he had usurped, and the notables of Quraish were made to witness to his words. Abu Sa'd then went to 'Abdul-Muttalib's house where he stayed for three nights, made 'Umra and left back for Madinah. Later on, Nawfal entered into alliance with Bani 'Abd Shams bin 'Abd Munaf against Bani Hashim. When Khuza'a, a tribe, saw Bani An-Najjar's support to 'Abdul-Muttalib they said: "He is our son as he is yours. We have more reasons to support him than you." 'Abd Munaf's mother was one of them. They went into An-Nadwa House and entered into alliance with Bani Hashim against Bani 'Abd Shams and Nawfal. It was an alliance that was later to constitute the main reason for the conquest of Makkah. 'Abdul-Muttalib witnessed two important events in his lifetime, namely digging Zamzam well and the Elephant raid.

In brief, 'Abdul-Muttalib received an order in his dream to dig Zamzam well in a particular place. He did that and found the things that Jurhum men had buried therein when they were forced to evacuate Makkah. He found the swords, armours and the two deer of gold. The gate of Al-Ka'bah was stamped from the gold swords and the two deer and then the tradition of providing Zamzam water to pilgrims was established.

When the well of Zamzam gushed water forth, Quraish made a claim to partnership in the enterprise, but 'Abdul-Muttalib refused their demands on grounds that Allâh had singled only him out for this honourable job. To settle the dispute, they agreed to consult Bani Sa'd's diviner. On their way, Allâh showed them His Signs that confirmed 'Abdul-Muttalib's prerogative as regards the sacred spring. Only then did 'Abdul-Muttalib make a solemn vow to sacrifice one of his adult children to Al-Ka'bah if he had ten.

The second event was that of Abraha As-Sabah Al-Habashi, the Abyssinian (Ethiopian) viceroy in Yemen. He had seen that the Arabs made their pilgrimage to Al-Ka'bah so he built a large church in San'a in order to attract the Arab pilgrims to it to the exclusion of Makkah. A man from Kinana tribe understood this move, therefore he entered the church stealthily at night and besmeared its front wall with excrement. When Abraha knew of that, he got very angry and led a great army – of sixty thousand warriors – to demolish Al-Ka'bah. He chose the biggest elephant for himself. His army included nine or thirteen elephants. He continued marching until he reached a place called Al-Magmas. There, he mobilized his army, prepared his elephants and got ready to enter Makkah. When he reached Muhassar Valley, between Muzdalifah and Mina, the elephant knelt down and refused to go forward. Whenever they directed it northwards, southwards or eastwards, the elephant moved quickly but when directed westwards towards Al-Ka'bah, it knelt down. Meanwhile, Allâh loosed upon them birds in flights, hurling against them stones of baked clay and made them like green blades devoured. These birds were very much like swallows and sparrows, each carrying three stones; one in its peak and two in its claws. The stones hit Abraha's men and cut their limbs and killed them. A large number of Abraha's soldiers were killed in this way and the others fled at random and died everywhere. Abraha himself had an infection that had his fingertips amputated. When he reached San'a he was in a miserable state and died soon after.

The Quraishites on their part had fled for their lives to the hillocks and mountain tops. When the enemy had been thus routed, they returned home safely. The Event of the Elephant took place in the month of Al-Muharram, fifty or fifty five days before the birth of Prophet Muhammad (Peace be upon him) which corresponded to late February or early March 571 A.D. It was a gift from Allâh to His Prophet and his family. It could actually be regarded as a Divine auspicious precursor of the light to come and accompany the advent of the Prophet and his family. By contrast, Jerusalem had suffered under the yoke of the atrocities of Allâh's enemies. Here we can recall Bukhtanassar in B.C. 587 and the Romans in 70 A.D. Al-Ka'bah, by Divine Grace, never came under the hold of the Christians – the Muslims of that time – although Makkah was populated by polytheists.

News of the Elephant Event reached the most distant corners of the then civilized world. Abyssinia (Ethiopia) maintained strong ties with the Romans, while the Persians on the other hand, were on the vigil with respect to any strategic changes that were looming on the socio- political horizon, and soon came to occupy Yemen. Incidentally, the Roman and Persian Empires stood for the powerful civilized world at that time. The Elephant Raid Event riveted the world's attention to the sacredness of Allâh's House, and showed that this House had been chosen by Allâh. It followed then if any of its people claimed Prophethood, it would be congruous with the outcome of the Elephant Event, and would provide a justifiable explanation for the ulterior Divine Wisdom that lay behind backing polytheists against Christians in a manner that transcended the cause-and-effect formula.

'Abdul-Muttalib had ten sons, Al-Harith, Az-Zubair, Abu Talib, 'Abdullah, Hamzah, Abu Lahab, Ghidaq, Maqwam, Safar and Al-'Abbas. He also had six daughters, who were Umm Al-Hakim – the only white one, Barrah, 'Atikah, Safiya, Arwa and Omaima.

4. 'Abdullah: The father of Prophet Muhammad (Peace be upon him). His mother was Fatimah, daughter of 'Amr bin 'A'idh bin 'Imran bin Makhzum bin Yaqdha bin Murra. 'Abdullah was the smartest of 'Abdul-Muttalib's sons, the chastest and the most loved. He was also the son whom the divination arrows pointed at to be slaughtered as a sacrifice to Al-Ka'bah.

When 'Abdul- Muttalib had ten sons and they reached maturity, he divulged to them his secret vow in which they silently and obediently acquiesced. Their names were written on divination arrows and given to the guardian of their most beloved goddess, Hubal. The arrows were shuffled and drawn. An arrow showed that it was 'Abdullah to be sacrificed. 'Abdul-Muttalib then took the boy to Al- Ka'bah with a razor to slaughter the boy. Quraish, his uncles from Makhzum tribe and his brother Abu Talib, however, tried to dissuade him from consummating his purpose. He then sought their advice as regards his vow.

They suggested that he summon a she-diviner to judge whereabout. She ordered that the divination arrows should be drawn with respect to 'Abdullah as well as ten camels. She added that drawing the lots should be repeated with ten more camels every time the arrow showed 'Abdullah. The operation was thus repeated until the number of the camels amounted to one hundred. At this point the arrow showed the camels, consequently they were all slaughtered (to the satisfaction of Hubal) instead of his son. The slaughtered camels were left for anyone to eat from, human or animal.

• This incident produced a change in the amount of blood-money usually accepted in Arabia. It had been ten camels, but after this event it was increased to a hundred. Islam, later on, approved of this. Another thing closely relevant to the above issue goes to the effect that the Prophet (Peace be upon him) once said:

"I am the offspring of the slaughtered two," meaning Ishmael and 'Abdullah. 'Abdul-Muttalib chose Amina, daughter of Wahab bin 'Abd Munaf bin Zahra bin Kilab, as a wife for his son, 'Abdullah. She thus, in the light of this ancestral lineage, stood eminent in respect of nobility of position and descent. Her father was the chief of Bani Zahra to whom great honour was attributed. They were married in Makkah, and soon after 'Abdullah was sent by his father to buy dates in Madinah where he died. In another version, 'Abdullah went to Syria on a trade journey and died in Madinah on his way back. He was buried in the house of An-Nabigha Al-Ju'di. He was twenty-five years old when he died. Most historians state that his death was two months before the birth of Muhammad (Peace Be Upon Him).

Some others said that his death was two months after the Prophet's birth. When Amina was informed of her husband's death, she celebrated his memory in a most heart-touching elegy. 'Abdullah left very little wealth — five camels, a small number of goats, a she-servant, called Barakah – Umm Aiman – who would later serve as the Prophet's nursemaid.

MUHAMMAD'S BIRTH AND FORTY YEARS PRIOR TO PROPHETHOOD

HIS BIRTH:

Muhammad (Peace be upon him), the Master of Prophets, was born in Bani Hashim lane in Makkah on Monday morning, the ninth of Rabi' Al-Awwal, the same year of the Elephant Event, and forty years of the reign of Kisra (Khosru Nushirwan), i.e. the twentieth or twenty-second of April, 571 A.D., according to the scholar Muhammad Sulaimân Al-Mansourpuri, and the astrologer Mahmûd Pasha.

Ibn Sa'd reported that Muhammad's mother said: "When he was born, there was a light that issued out of my pudendum and lit the palaces of Syria." Ahmad reported on the authority of 'Arbadh bin Sariya something similar to this. It was but controversially reported that significant precursors accompanied his birth: fourteen galleries of Kisra's palace cracked and rolled down, the Magians' sacred fire died down and some churches on Lake Sawa sank down and collapsed.

His mother immediately sent someone to inform his grandfather 'Abdul-Muttalib of the happy event. Happily he came to her, carried him to Al-Ka'bah, prayed to Allâh and thanked Him. 'Abdul-Muttalib called the baby Muhammad, a name not then common among the Arabs. He circumcised him on his seventh day as was the custom of the Arabs.

The first woman who suckled him after his mother was Thuyebah, the concubine of Abu Lahab, with her son, Masrouh. She had suckled Hamzah bin 'Abdul-Muttalib before and later Abu Salamah bin 'Abd Al-Asad Al-Makhzumi.

BABYHOOD:

It was the general custom of the Arabs living in towns to send their children away to bedouin wet nurses so that they might grow up in the free and healthy surroundings of the desert whereby they would develop a robust frame and acquire the pure speech and manners of the bedouins, who were noted both for chastity of their language and for being free from those vices which usually develop in sedentary societies. The Prophet (Peace be upon him) was later entrusted to Haleemah bint Abi Dhuaib from Bani Sa'd bin Bakr. Her husband was Al-Harith bin 'Abdul 'Uzza called Abi Kabshah, from the same tribe.

Muhammad (Peace be upon him) had several foster brothers and sisters, 'Abdullah bin Al-Harith, Aneesah bint Al-Harith, Hudhafah or Judhamah bint Al-Harith (known as Ash-Shayma'), and she used to nurse the Prophet (Peace be upon him) and Abu Sufyan bin Al-Harith bin 'Abdul-Muttalib, the Prophet's cousin. Hamzah bin 'Abdul-Muttalib, the Prophet's uncle, was suckled by the same two wet nurses, Thuyeba and Haleemah As-Sa'diyah, who suckled the Prophet (Peace be upon him).

Traditions delightfully relate how Haleemah and the whole of her household were favoured by successive strokes of good fortune while the baby Muhammad (Peace be upon him) lived under her care. Ibn Ishaq states that Haleemah narrated that she along with her husband and a suckling babe, set out from her village in the company of some women of her clan in quest of children to suckle.

She said: It was a year of drought and famine and we had nothing to eat. I rode on a brown she-ass. We also had with us an old she-camel. By Allâh we could not get even a drop of milk. We could not have a wink of sleep during the night for the child kept crying on account of hunger. There was not enough milk in my breast and even the she-camel had nothing to feed him. We used to constantly pray for rain and immediate relief. At length we reached Makkah looking for children to suckle.

Not even a single woman amongst us accepted the Messenger of Allâh (Peace be upon him) offered to her. As soon as they were told that he was an orphan, they refused him. We had fixed our eyes on the reward that we would get from the child's father. An orphan! What are his grandfather and mother likely to do? So we spurned him because of that. Every woman who came with me got a suckling and when we were about to depart, I said to my husband: "By Allâh, I do not like to go back along with the other women without any baby. I should go to that orphan and I must take him." He said, "There is no harm in doing so and perhaps Allâh might bless us through him." So I went and took him because there was simply no other alternative left for me but to take him. When I lifted him in my arms and returned to my place I put him on my breast and to my great surprise, I found enough milk in it. He drank to his heart's content, and so did his foster brother and then both of them went to sleep although my baby had not been able to sleep the previous night. My husband then went to the she-camel to milk it and, to his astonishment, he found plenty of milk in it. He milked it and we drank to our fill, and enjoyed a sound sleep during the night. The next morning, my husband said: "By Allâh Haleemah, you must understand that you have been able to get a blessed child." And I replied: "By the grace of Allâh, I hope so."

The tradition is explicit on the point that Haleemah's return journey and her subsequent life, as long as the Prophet (Peace be upon him) stayed with her, was encircled with a halo of good fortune. The donkey that she rode when she came to Makkah was lean and almost foundered; it recovered speed much to the amazement of Haleemah's fellow travellers. By the time they reached the encampments in the country of the clan of Sa'd, they found the scales of fortune turned in their favour. The barren land sprouted forth luxuriant grass and beasts came back to them satisfied and full of milk.

Muhammad (Peace be upon him) stayed with Haleemah for two years until he was weaned as Haleemah said: We then took him back to his mother requesting her earnestly to have him stay with us and benefit by the good fortune and blessings he had brought us. We persisted in our request which we substantiated by our anxiety over the child catching a certain infection peculiar to Makkah. At last, we were granted our wish and the Prophet (Peace be upon him) stayed with us until he was four or five years of age.

When, as related by Anas in Sahih Muslim, Gabriel came down and ripped his chest open and took out the heart. He then extracted a blood-clot out of it and said: "That was the part of Satan in thee." And then he washed it with the water of Zamzam in a gold basin. After that the heart was joined together and restored to its place. The boys and playmates came running to his mother, i.e. his nurse, and said:

"Verily, Muhammad (Peace be upon him) has been murdered." They all rushed towards him and found him all right only his face was white.

BACK TO HIS COMPASSIONATE MOTHER:

After this event, Haleemah was worried about the boy and returned him to his mother with whom he stayed until he was six.

In respect of the memory of her late husband, Amina decided to visit his grave in Yathrib (Madinah). She set out to cover a journey of 500 kilometers with her orphan boy, woman servant Umm Ayman and her father-in-law 'Abdul-Muttalib. She spent a month there and then took her way back to Makkah. On the way, she had a severe illness and died in Abwa on the road between Makkah and Madinah.

BACK TO HIS COMPASSIONATE GRANDFATHER:

'Abdul-Muttalib brought the boy to Makkah. He had warm passions towards the boy, his orphan grandson, whose recent disaster (his mother's death) added more to the pains of the past. 'Abdul-Muttalib was more passionate with his grandson than with his own children. He never left the boy a prey to loneliness, but always preferred him to his own kids. Ibn Hisham reported: A mattress was put in the shade of Al-Ka'bah for 'Abdul-Muttalib. His children used to sit around that mattress in honour to their father, but Muhammad (Peace be upon him) used to sit on it.

His uncles would take him back, but if 'Abdul-Muttalib was present, he would say: "Leave my grandson. I swear by Allâh that this boy will hold a significant position." He used to seat the boy on his mattress, pat his back and was always pleased with what the boy did.

When Muhammad (Peace be upon him) was eight years, two months and ten days old, his grandfather 'Abdul-Muttalib passed away in Makkah. The charge of the Prophet (Peace be upon him) was now passed on to his uncle Abu Talib, who was the brother of the Prophet's father.

Abu Talib took the charge of his nephew in the best way. He put him with his children and preferred him to them. He singled the boy out with great respect and high esteem. Abu Talib remained for forty years cherishing his nephew and extending all possible protection and support to him. His relations with the others were determined in the light of the treatment they showed to the Prophet (Peace be upon him). Ibn 'Asakir reported on the authority of Jalhamah bin 'Arfuta who said: "I came to Makkah when it was a rainless year, so Quraish said 'O Abu Talib, the valley has become leafless and the children hungry, let us go and pray for rain-fall.' Abu Talib went to Al-Ka'bah with a young boy who was as beautiful as the sun, and a black cloud was over his head. Abu Talib and the boy stood by the wall of Al-Ka'bah and prayed for rain. Immediately clouds from all directions gathered and rain fell heavily and caused the flow of springs and growth of plants in the town and the country.

BAHIRA, THE MONK:

When the Messenger of Allâh (Peace be upon him) was twelve years old, he went with his uncle Abu Talib on a business journey to Syria. When they reached Busra (which was a part of Syria, in the vicinity of Howran under the Roman domain) they met a monk called Bahira (his real name was Georges), who showed great kindness, and entertained them lavishly. He had never been in the habit of receiving or entertaining them before. He readily enough recognized the Prophet (Peace be upon him) and said while taking his hand:

"This is the master of all humans. Allâh will send him with a Message which will be a mercy to all beings." Abu Talib asked: "How do you know that?" He replied: "When you appeared from the direction of 'Aqabah, all stones and trees prostrated themselves, which they never do except for a Prophet. I can recognize him also by the seal of Prophethood which is below his shoulder, like an apple. We have got to learn this from our books." He also asked Abu Talib to send the boy back to Makkah and not to take him to Syria for fear of the Jews. Abu Talib obeyed and sent him back to Makkah with some of his men servants.

THE 'SACRILIGIOUS' WARS:

Muhammad (Peace be upon him) was hardly fifteen when the 'sacrilegious' wars — which continued with varying fortunes and considerable loss of human life for a number of years — broke out between Quraish and Banu Kinana on the one side and Qais 'Ailan tribe on the other. It was thus called because the inviolables were made violable, the prohibited months being included. Harb bin Omaiyah, on account of his outstanding position and honourable descent, used to be the leader of Quraish and their allies. In one of those battles, the Prophet (Peace be upon him) attended on his uncles but did not raise arms against their opponents. His efforts were confined to picking up the arrows of the enemy as they fell, and handing them over to his uncles.

ALFUDOUL CONFEDERACY:

At the conclusion of these wars, when peace was restored, people felt the need for forming confederacy at Makkah for suppressing violence and injustice, and vindicating the rights of the weak and the destitute. Representatives of Banu Hashim, Banu Al-Muttalib, Asad bin 'Abd Al-'Uzza, Zahrah bin Kilab and Taim bin Murra were called to meet in the habitation of an honourable elderly man called 'Abdullah bin Jada'an At-Taimy to enter into a confederacy that would provide for the above-mentioned items.

The Messenger of Allâh (Peace be upon him) shortly after he had been honoured with the ministry of Prophethood, witnessed this league and commented on it, with very positive words: "I witnessed a confederacy in the house of 'Abdullah bin Jada'an. It was more appealing to me than herds of cattle. Even now in the period of Islam I would respond positively to attending such a meeting if I were invited."

In fact, the spirit of this confederacy and the course of deliberations therein marked a complete departure from the pre-Islamic tribal-pride. The story that led to its convention says that a man from Zubaid clan came as a merchant to Makkah where he sold some commodities to Al-'As bin Wail As-Sahmy. The latter by hook or by crook tried to evade paying for the goods. The salesman sought help from the different clans in Quraish but they paid no heed to his earnest pleas. He then resorted to a mountain top and began, at the top of his voice, to recite verses of complaint giving account of the injustices he sustained. Az-Zubair bin 'Abdul-Muttalib heard of him and made inquiries into the matter. Consequently, the parties to the aforesaid confederacy convened their meeting and managed to force Az-Zubaidy's money out of Al-'As bin Wa'il.

MUHAMMAD'S EARLY JOB:

Muhammad (Peace be upon him), had no particular job at his early youth, but it was reported that he worked as a shepherd for Bani Sa'd and in Makkah. At the age of 25, he went to Syria as a merchant for Khadijah (May Allah be pleased with her) Ibn Ishaq reported that Khadijah, daughter of Khwailid was a business-woman of great honour and fortune. She used to employ men to do her business for a certain percentage of the profits. Quraish people were mostly tradespeople, so when Khadijah was informed of Muhammad (Peace be upon him), his truthful words, great honesty and kind manners, she sent for him. She offered him money to go to Syria and do her business, and she would give him a higher rate than the others. She would also send her hireling, Maisarah, with him. He agreed and went with her servant to Syria for trade.

HIS MARRIEAGE TO KHADIJAH:

When he returned to Makkah, Khadijah noticed, in her money, more profits and blessings than she used to. Her hireling also told her of Muhammad's good manners, honesty, deep thought, sincerity and faith. She realized that she homed at her target. Many prominent men had asked for her hand in marriage but she always spurned their advances. She disclosed her wish to her friend Nafisa, daughter of Maniya, who immediately went to Muhammad (Peace be upon him) and broke the good news to him. He agreed and requested his uncles to go to Khadijah's uncle and talk on this issue. Subsequently, they were married. The marriage contract was witnessed by Bani Hashim and the heads of Mudar. This took place after the Prophet's return from Syria. He gave her twenty camels as dowry. She was, then, forty years old and was considered as the best woman of her folk in lineage, fortune and wisdom. She was the first woman whom the Messenger of Allâh (Peace be upon him) married. He did not get married to any other until she had died.

Khadijah bore all his children, except Ibrahim: Al-Qasim, Zainab, Ruqaiyah, Umm Kulthum, Fatimah and 'Abdullah who was called Taiyib and Tahir. All his sons died in their childhood and all the daughters except Fatimah died during his lifetime. Fatimah died six months after his death. All his daughters witnessed Islam, embraced it, and emigrated to Madinah.

REBUILDING AL-KA'BAH AND THE ARBITRATION ISSUE:

When the Messenger of Allâh (Peace be upon him) was thirty five, Quraish started rebuilding Al-Ka'bah. That was because it was a low building of white stones no more than 6.30 metres high, from the days of Ishmael. It was also roofless and that gave the thieves easy access to its treasures inside. It was also exposed to the wearing factors of nature — because it was built a long time ago — that weakened and cracked its walls. Five years before Prophethood, there was a great flood in Makkah that swept towards Al-Ka'bah and almost demolished it.

Quraish was obliged to rebuild it to safeguard its holiness and position. The chiefs of Quraish decided to use only licit money in rebuilding Al-Ka'bah, so all money that derived from harlotry, usury or unjust practices was excluded. They were, at first, too awed to knock down the wall, but Al-Waleed bin Al-Mugheerah Al-Mukhzumi started the work. Seeing that no harm had happened to him, the others participated in demolishing the walls until they reached the basis laid by Abraham. When they started rebuilding its walls, they divided the work among the tribes. Each tribe was responsible for rebuilding a part of it. The tribes collected stones. The man who laid the stones was a Roman mason called Baqum. The work went on in harmony till the time came to put the sacred Black Stone in its proper place. Then strife broke out among the chiefs, and lasted for four or five days, each contesting for the honour of placing the stone in its position. Daggers were on the point of being drawn and great bloodshed seemed imminent. Luckily, the oldest among the chiefs Abu Omaiyah bin Mugheerah Al-Makhzumi made a proposal which was accepted by all. He said: "Let him, who enters the Sanctuary first of all, decide on the point." It was then Allâh's Will that the Messenger of Allâh (Peace be upon him) should be the first to enter the Mosque.

On seeing him, all the people on the scene, cried with one voice: "Al-Ameen (the trustworthy) has come. We are content to abide by his decision." Calm and self-possessed, Muhammad (Peace be upon him) received the commission and at once resolved upon an expedient which was to conciliate them all. He asked for a mantle which he spread on the ground and placed the stone in its center. He then asked the representatives of the different clans among them, to lift the stone all together. When it had reached the proper place, Muhammad (Peace be upon him) laid it in the proper position with his own hands. This is how a very tense situation was eased and a grave danger averted by the wisdom of the Prophet (Peace be upon him).

Quraish ran short of the licit money, they collected, so they eliminated six yards area on the northern side of Al-Ka'bah which is called Al-Hijr or Al-Hateem.

They raised its door two metres from the level ground to let in only the people whom they desired. When the structure was fifteen yards high they erected the roof which rested on six columns.

When the building of Al-Ka'bah had finished, it assumed a square form fifteen metres high. The side with the Black Stone and the one opposite were ten metres long each. The Black Stone was 1.50 metre from the circumambulation level ground. The two other sides were twelve metres long each. The door was two metres high from the level ground. A building structure of 0.25 metre high and 0.30 metre wide on the average surrounded Al-Ka'bah. It was called Ash-Shadherwan, originally an integral part of the Sacred Sanctuary, but Quraish left it out.

A RAPID REVIEW OF MUHAMMAD'S BIOGRAPHY BEFORE COMMISSIONING OF THE PROPHETHOOD:

Prophet Muhammad (Peace be upon him) was, in his youth, a combination of the best social attributes. He was an exemplary man and faultless insight. He was favoured with intelligence, originality of thought and accurate choice of the means leading to accurate goals. His long silence helped favourably in his habit of meditation and deep investigation into the truth. His vivid mind and pure nature were helpfully instrumental in assimilating and comprehending ways of life and people, individual and community-wise. He shunned superstitious practices but took an active part in constructive and useful dealings, otherwise, he would have recourse to his self-consecrated solitude. He kept himself aloof from drinking wine, eating meat slaughtered on stone altars, or attending idolatrous festivals. He held the idols in extreme aversion and most abhorrence. He could never tolerate someone swearing by Al-Lat and Al-'Uzza. Allâh's providence, no doubts, detached him from all abominable or evil practices. Even when he tried to obey his instinct to enjoy some life pleasures or follow some irrespectable traditions, Allâh's providence intervened to curb any lapse in this course.

Ibn Al-Atheer reported Muhammad (Peace be upon him) as saying: "I have never tried to do what my people do except for two times. Every time Allâh intervened and checked me from doing so and I never did that again. Once I told my fellow-shepherd to take care of my sheep when we were in the upper part of Makkah. I wanted to go down to Makkah and entertain myself as the young men did. I went down to the first house of Makkah where I heard music. I entered and asked: 'What is this?' Someone answered: 'It is a wedding party.' I sat down and listened but soon went into deep sleep. I was awakened by the heat of the sun. I went back to my fellow-shepherd and told him of what had happened to me. I have never tried it again."

Al-Bukhari reported on the authority of Jabir bin 'Abdullah that he said: "While the people were rebuilding Al-Ka'bah, the Prophet Muhammad (Peace be upon him) went with 'Abbas to carry some stones. 'Abbas said: 'Put your loincloth round your neck to protect you from the stones.' (As he did that) the Prophet (Peace be upon him) fell to the ground and his eyes turned skyward. Later on he woke up and shouted: 'My loincloth... my loincloth.' He wrapped himself in his loincloth." In another report: "His loins were never seen afterwards."

The authorities agree in ascribing to the youth of Muhammad (Peace be upon him) modesty of deportment, virtuous behaviour and graceful manners. He proved himself to be the ideal of manhood, and to possess a spotless character. He was the most obliging to his compatriots, the most honest in his talk and the mildest in temper. He was the most gentle-hearted, chaste, hospitable and always impressed people by his piety-inspiring countenance. He was the most truthful and the best to keep covenant. His fellow-citizens, by common consent, gave him the title of Al-'Ameen (trustworthy). The Mother of believers, Khadijah (May Allah be pleased with her) once said: He unites uterine relations, he helps the poor and the needy, he entertains the guests and endures hardships in the path of truthfulness.

IN THE SHADE OF THE MESSAGE AND PROPHETHOOD IN THE CAVE HIRA:

When Prophet Muhammad (Peace be upon him) was nearly forty, he had been wont to pass long hours in retirement meditating and speculating over all aspects of creation around him. This meditative temperament helped to widen the mental gap between him and his compatriots. He used to provide himself with Sawiq (barley porridge) and water and then directly head for the hills and ravines in the neighbourhood of Makkah. One of these in particular was his favourite resort — a cave named Hira', in the Mount An-Nour. It was only two miles from Makkah, a small cave 4 yards long and 1.75 yard wide. He would always go there and invite wayfarers to share him his modest provision. He used to devote most of his time, and Ramadan in particular, to worship and meditation on the universe around him. His heart was restless about the moral evils and idolatry that were rampant among his people; he was as yet helpless because no definite course, or specific approach had been available for him to follow and rectify the ill practices around him. This solitude attended with this sort of contemplative approach must be understood in its Divine perspective. It was a preliminary stage to the period of grave responsibilities that he was to shoulder very soon.

Privacy and detachment from the impurities of life were two indispensable prerequisites for the Prophet's soul to come into close communion with the Unseen Power that lies behind all aspects of existence in this infinite universe. It was a rich period of privacy which lasted for three years and ushered in a new era, of indissoluble contact with that Power.

GAGRIEL BRINGS DOWN THE REVELATION:

When he was forty, the age of complete perfection at which Prophets were always ordered to disclose their Message, signs of his Prophethood started to appear and twinkle on the horizons of life; they were the true visions he used to experience for six months. The period of Prophethood was 23 years; so the period of these six months of true visions constituted an integral part of the forty-six parts of Prophethood.

In Ramadan, in his third year of solitude in the cave of Hira', Allâh's Will desired His mercy to flow on earth and Muhammad (Peace be upon him) was honoured with Prophethood, and the light of Revelation burst upon him with some verses of the Noble Qur'ân.

As for the exact date, careful investigation into circumstantial evidence and relevant clues point directly to Monday, 21st. Ramadan at night, i.e. Au, 10, 610 A.D. with Prophet Muhammad (Peace be upon him) exactly 40 years, 6 months and 12 days of age, i.e. 39 Gregorian years, 3 months and 22 days. 'Aishah, the veracious, gave the following narration of that most significant event that brought the Divine light which would dispel the darkness of disbelief and ignorance. It led life down a new course and brought about the most serious amendment to the line of the history of mankind:

Forerunners of the Revelation assumed the form of true visions that would strikingly come true all the time. After that, solitude became dear to him and he would go to the cave, Hira', to engage in Tahannuth (devotion) there for a certain number of nights before returning to his family, and then he would return for provisions for a similar stay.

At length, unexpectedly, the Truth (the angel) came to him and said, "Recite." "I cannot recite," he [Muhammad (Peace be upon him)] said.

The Prophet (Peace be upon him) described: "Then he took me and squeezed me vehemently and then let me go and repeated the order 'Recite.' 'I cannot recite' said I, and once again he squeezed me and let me till I was exhausted. Then he said: 'Recite.' I said 'I cannot recite.' He squeezed me for a third time and then let me go and said:

• "Read! In the Name of your Lord, Who has created (all that exists), has created man from a clot (a piece of thick coagulated blood). Read! And your Lord is the Most Generous.'" [96:1-3]

$$ \text{اقْرَأْ بِاسْمِ رَبِّكَ الَّذِي خَلَقَ ﴿١﴾} $$

$$ \text{خَلَقَ الْإِنْسَانَ مِنْ عَلَقٍ ﴿٢﴾} $$

$$ \text{اقْرَأْ وَرَبُّكَ الْأَكْرَمُ ﴿٣﴾} $$

The Prophet (Peace be upon him) repeated these verses. He was trembling with fear. At this stage, he came back to his wife Khadijah, and said, "Cover me, ... cover me." They covered him until he restored security. He apprised Khadijah of the incident of the cave and added that he was horrified. His wife tried to soothe him and reassured him saying, "Allâh will never disgrace you. You unite uterine relations; you bear the burden of the weak; you help the poor and the needy, you entertain the guests and endure hardships in the path of truthfulness."

She set out with the Prophet (Peace be upon him) to her cousin Waraqa bin Nawfal bin Asad bin 'Abd Al-'Uzza, who had embraced Christianity in the pre-Islamic period, and used to write the Bible in Hebrew. He was a blind old man. Khadijah said: "My cousin! Listen to your nephew!" Waraqa said: "O my nephew! What did you see?"

The Messenger of Allâh (Peace be upon him) told him what had happened to him. Waraqa replied: "This is 'Namus' i.e. (the angel who is entrusted with Divine Secrets) that Allâh sent to Moses. I wish I were younger. I wish I could live up to the time when your people would turn you out." Muhammad (Peace be upon him) asked: "Will they drive me out?" Waraqa answered in the affirmative and said: "Anyone who came with something similar to what you have brought was treated with hostility; and if I should be alive till that day, then I would support you strongly." A few days later Waraqa died and the revelation also subsided.

At-Tabari and Ibn Hisham reported that the Messenger of Allâh (Peace be upon him) left the cave of Hira' after being surprised by the Revelation, but later on, returned to the cave and continued his solitude. Afterwards, he came back to Makkah. At-Tabari reported on this incident, saying:

After mentioning the coming of the Revelation, the Messenger of Allâh (Peace be upon him) said: "I have never abhorred anyone more than a poet or a mad man. I cannot stand looking at either of them. I will never tell anyone of Quraish of my Revelation. I will climb a mountain and throw myself down and die. That will relieve me. I went to do that but halfway up the mountain, I heard a voice from the sky saying 'O Muhammad! You are the Messenger of Allâh (Peace be upon him) and I am Gabriel.' I looked upwards and saw Gabriel in the form of a man putting his legs on the horizon. He said: 'O Muhammad You are the Messenger of Allâh (Peace be upon him) and I am Gabriel.' I stopped and looked at him. His sight distracted my attention from what I had intended to do. I stood in my place transfixed. I tried to shift my eyes away from him. He was in every direction I looked at. I stopped in my place without any movement until Khadijah sent someone to look for me. He went down to Makkah and came back while I was standing in the same place. Gabriel then left, and I went back home. I found Khadijah at home, so I sat very close to her. She asked: 'Father of Al-Qasim! Where have you been? I sent someone to look for you. He went to Makkah and returned to me.' I told her of what I had seen. She replied: 'It is a propitious sign, O my husband. Pull yourself together, I swear by Allâh that you are a Messenger for this nation.' Then she stood up and went to Waraqa and informed him. Waraqa said: 'I swear by Allâh that he has received the same Namus, i.e. angel that was sent to Moses. He is the Prophet of this nation. Tell him to be patient.' She came back to him and told him of Waraqa's words. When the Messenger of Allâh (Peace be upon him) finished his solitary stay and went down to Makkah, he went to Waraqa, who told him: 'You are the Prophet of this nation. I swear by Allâh that you have received the same angel that was sent to Moses.'"

INTERRUPION OF REVELATION:

Ibn Sa'd reported on the authority of Ibn 'Abbas that the Revelation paused for a few days. After careful study, this seems to be the most possible. To say that it lasted for three and a half years, as some scholars allege, is not correct, but here there is no room to go into more details. Meanwhile, the Prophet (Peace be upon him), was caught in a sort of depression coupled with astonishment and perplexity. Al-Bukhari reported: The Divine inspiration paused for a while and the Prophet (Peace be upon him) became so sad, as we have heard, that he intended several times to throw himself from the tops of high mountains, and every time he went up the top of a mountain in order to throw himself down, Gabriel would appear before him and say: "O Muhammad! You are indeed Allâh's Messenger in truth," whereupon his heart would become quiet and he would calm down and return home. Whenever the period of the coming of the Revelation used to become long, he would do as before, but Gabriel would appear again before him and say to him what he had said before.

ONCE, GABRIEL BRINGS ALLAH'S REVELATION:

Ibn Hajar said: 'That (the pause of Allâh's revelation for a few days) was to relieve the Messenger of Allâh (Peace be upon him) of the fear he experienced and to make him long for the Revelation. When the shades of puzzle receded, the flags of truth were raised, the Messenger of Allâh (Peace be upon him) knew for sure that he had become the Messenger of the Great Lord. He was also certain that what had come to him was no more than the ambassador of inspiration. His waiting and longing for the coming of the revelation constituted a good reason for his steadfastness and self-possession on the arrival of Allâh's inspiration, Al-Bukhari reported on the authority of Jabir bin 'Abdullah that he had heard the Messenger of Allâh (Peace be upon him) speak about the period of pause as follows:

"While I was walking, I heard a voice from the sky. I looked up, and surely enough, it was the same angel who had visited me in the cave of Hira'. He was sitting on a chair between the earth and the sky. I was very afraid of him and knelt on the ground. I went home saying: 'Cover me ..., Cover me ...'. Allâh revealed to me the verses:

• O you [Muhammad (Peace be upon him)] enveloped (in garments)! Arise and warn! And your Lord (Allâh) magnify! And your garments purify! And keep away from Ar-Rujz (the idols)!'" [74:1-5]

After that the revelation started coming strongly, frequently and regularly.

SOME DETAILS PERTINENT TO THE SUCCESSIVE STAGES OF REVELATION:

Before we go into the details of the period of communicating the Message and Prophethood, we would like to get acquainted with the stages of the Revelation which constituted the main source of the Message and the subject-matter of the Call. Ibn Al-Qayyim, mentioning the stages of the Revelation, said:

- The First: The period of true vision. It was the starting point of the Revelation to the Men of Allâh (Peace be upon him).

The Second: What the angel invisibly cast in the Prophet's mind and heart. The Messenger of Allâh (Peace be upon him) said: "The Noble Spirit revealed to me 'No soul will perish until it exhausts its due course, so fear Allâh and gently request Him. Never get so impatient to the verge of disobedience of Allâh. What Allâh has can never be acquired but through obedience to Him.'"

The Third: The angel used to visit the Messenger of Allâh (Peace be upon him) in the form of a human being and would speak to him directly. This would enable him to fully understand what the angel said. The angel was sometimes seen in this form by the Prophet's Companions.

The Fourth: The angel came to him like the toll of a bell and this was the most difficult form because the angel used to seize him tightly and sweat would stream from his forehead even on the coldest day. If the Prophet (Peace be upon him) was on his camel, the camel would not withstand the weight, so it would immediately kneel down on the ground. Once the Messenger of Allâh (Peace be upon him) had such a revelation when he was sitting and his thigh was on Zaid's, Zaid felt the pressure had almost injured his thigh.

The Fifth: The Prophet (Peace be upon him) saw the angel in his actual form. The angel would reveal to him what Allâh had ordered him to reveal. This, as mentioned in (Qur'ân), in Sûrah An-Najm (Chapter 53 - The Star), happened twice.

The Sixth: What Allâh Himself revealed to him in heaven i.e. when he ascended to heaven and received Allâh's behest of Salât (prayer).

The Seventh: Allâh's Words to His Messenger (Peace be upon him) at first hand without the mediation of an angel. It was a privilege granted to Moses (Peace be upon him) and clearly attested in the Qur'ân, as it is attested to our Prophet (Peace be upon him) in the Sûrah Al-Isrâ' (Chapter 17 - The Journey by Night) of the Noble Qur'ân.

Some religious scholars added a controversial eighth stage in which they state that Allâh spoke to the Prophet (Peace be upon him) directly without a curtain in between. This issue remains however unconfirmed.

PROCLAIMING ALLAH, THE ALL-HIGH; AND THE IMMEDIATE CONSTITUENTS

The first Revelation sent to the Prophet (Peace be upon him) implied several injunctions, simple in form but highly effective and of serious far-reaching ramifications. The angel communicated to him a manifest Message saying:

• "O you [Muhammad (Peace be upon him)] enveloped (in garments)! Arise and warn! And your Lord (Allâh) magnify! And your garments purify! And keep away from Ar-Rujz (the idols). And give not a thing in order to have more (or consider not your deeds of Allâh's obedience as a favour to Allâh). And be patient for the sake of your Lord (i.e. perform your duty to Allâh)!" [74:1-7]

For convenience and ease of understanding, we are going to segment the Message into its immediate constituents:

1. The ultimate objective of warning is to make sure that no one breaching the pleasures of Allâh in the whole universe is ignorant of the serious consequences that his behaviour entails, and to create a sort of unprecedented shock within his mind and heart.

2. 'Magnifying the Lord' dictates explicitly that the only pride allowed to nourish on the earth is exclusively Allâh's to the exclusion of all the others'.

3. 'Cleansing the garments and shunning all aspects of abomination' point directly to the indispensable need to render both the exterior and interior exceptionally chaste and pure, in addition to the prerequisite of sanctifying the soul and establishing it highly immune against the different sorts of impurities and the various kinds of pollutants. Only through this avenue can the soul of the Prophet (Peace be upon him) reach an ideal status and become eligible to enjoy the shady mercy of Allâh and His protection, security, guidance and ever-shining light; and will consequently set the highest example to the human community, attract the sound hearts and inspire awe and reverence in the stray ones in such a manner that all the world, in agreement or disagreement, will head for it and take it as the rock-bed in all facets of their welfare.

4. The Prophet (Peace be upon him) must not regard his strife in the way of Allâh as a deed of grace that entitles him to a great reward. On the contrary, he has to exert himself to the utmost, dedicate his whole efforts and be ready to offer all sacrifices in a spirit of self-fogetfulness enveloped by an ever-present awareness of Allâh, without the least sense of pride in his deeds or sacrifices.

5. The last verse of the Qur'ân revealed to the Prophet (Peace be upon him) alludes to the hostile attitude of the obdurate disbelievers, who will jeer at him and his followers. They are expected to disparage him and step up their malice to the point of scheming against his life and lives of all the believers around him. In this case he has got to be patient and is supposed to persevere and display the highest degree of stamina for the sole purpose of attaining the pleasure of Allâh.

These were the basic preliminaries that the Prophet (Peace be upon him) had to observe, very simple injunctions in appearance, greatly fascinating in their calm rhythm, but highly effective in practice. They constituted the trigger that aroused a far-ranging tempest in all the corners of the world.

The verses comprise the constituents of the new call and propagation of the new faith. A warning logically implies that there are malpractices with painful consequences to be sustained by the perpetrators, and since the present life is not necessarily the only room to bring people to account for their misdeeds or some of them, then the warning would necessarily imply calling people to account on another day, i.e. the Day of Resurrection, and this per se suggests the existence of a life other than this one we are living. All the verses of the Noble Qur'ân call people to testify explicitly to the Oneness of Allâh, to delegate all their affairs to Allâh, the All-High, and to subordinate the desires of the self and the desires of Allâh's servants to the attainment of His Pleasures.

The constituents of the call to Islam could, briefly speaking, go as follows:

1. Testimony to the Oneness of Allâh.

2. Belief in the Hereafter.

3. Sanctifying one's soul and elevating it high above evils and abominations that conduce to terrible consequences, besides this, there is the dire need for virtues and perfect manners coupled with habituating oneself to righteous deeds.

4. Committing one's all affairs to Allâh, the All-High.

5. All the foregoing should run as a natural corollary to unwavering belief in Muhammad's Message, and abidance by his noble leadership and righteous guidance.

The verses have been prefaced, in the voice of the Most High, by a heavenly call mandating the Prophet (Peace be upon him) to undertake this daunting responsibility (calling people unto Allâh). The verses meant to extract him forcibly out of his sleep, divest him of his mantle and detach him from the warmth and quiet of life, and then drive him down a new course attended with countless hardships, and requiring a great deal of strife in the way of Allâh:

- "O you [Muhammad (Peace be upon him)] enveloped (in garments)! Arise and warn." [74:1-2] Suggesting that to live to oneself is quite easy, but it has been decided that you have to shoulder this heavy burden; consequently sleep, comfort, or warm bed are items decreed to be alien in your lexicon of life. O Muhammad, arise quickly for the strife and toil awaiting you; no time is there for sleep and such amenities; grave responsibilities have been Divinely determined to fall to your lot, and drive you into the turmoil of life to develop a new sort of precarious affinity with the conscience of people and the reality of life. The Prophet (Peace be upon him) managed quite successfully to rise to his feet and measure up to the new task, he went ahead in a spirit of complete selflessness, relentlessly striving and never abating in carrying the burden of the great Trust, the burden of enlightening mankind, and the heavy weight of the new faith and strife for over twenty years, nothing distracting his attention from his mission. May Allâh reward him, for us and all humanity, the best in the afterlife. The following research at hand gives an account in miniature of his long strive and uninterrupted struggle he made after receiving the ministry of Messengership.

PHASES ANS STAGES OF THE CALL:

The Muhammadan Call could be divided into two phases distinctively demarcated:

1. The Makkan phase: nearly thirteen years.

2. The Madinese phase: fully ten years.

Each of the two phases included distinctive features easily discernible through accurate scrutiny into the circumstances that characterized each of them. The Makkan phase can be divided into three stages:

1. The stage of the secret Call: three years.

2. The stage of the proclamation of the Call in Makkah: from the beginning of the fourth year of Prophethood to almost the end of the tenth year.

3. The stage of the call to Islam and propagating it beyond Makkah: it lasted from the end of tenth year of the Prophethood until Muhammad's (Peace be upon him) emigration to Madinah. The Madinese phase will be considered later in its due course.

THE FIRST STAGE

STRIFE IN THE WAY OF THE CALL THREE YEARS OF SECRETE CALL:

It is well-known that Makkah was the centre for the Arabs, and housed the custodians of Al-Ka'bah. Protection and guardianship of the idols and stone graven images that received veneration on the part of all the Arabs lay in the hands of the Makkans. Hence the difficulty of hitting the target of reform and rectitude in a place considered the den of idolatry. Working in such an atmosphere no doubt requires unshakable will and determination that is why the call unto Islam assumed a clandestine form so that the Makkans should not be enraged by the unexpected surprise.

THE EARLY CONVERTS:

The Prophet (Peace be upon him) naturally initiated his sacred mission right from home and then moved to the people closely associated with him. He called unto Islam whomsoever he thought would attest the truth which had come from his Lord. In fact, a host of people who nursed not the least seed of doubt as regards the Prophet (Peace be upon him), immediately responded and quite readily embraced the true faith. They are known in the Islamic literature as the early converts. Khadijah, the Prophet's spouse, the mother of believers, was the first to enter the fold of Islam followed by his freed slave Zaid bin Harithah, his cousin, 'Ali bin Abi Talib, who had been living with him since his early childhood, and next came his intimate friend Abu Bakr As-Siddiq (Abu Bakr the truth verifier). All of those professed Islam on the very first day of the call.

Abu Bakr, and from the first day he embraced Islam, proved to be an energetic and most zealous activist. He was wealthy, obliging, mild and upright.

People used to frequent his house and draw nigh to him for his knowledge, amity, pleasant company and business. He invited whomever he had confidence in to Islam and through his personal efforts a good number of people converted to Islam, such as 'Uthman bin 'Affan Al-Umawi, Az-Zubair bin 'Awwam Al-Asadi, 'Abdur Rahman bin 'Awf, Sa'd bin Abi Waqqas, Az-Zuhri and Talhah bin 'Ubaidullah At-Tamimy. Those eight men constituted the forerunners and more specifically the vanguard of the new faith in Arabia. Among the early Muslim were Bilal bin Rabah (the Abyssinian), Abu 'Ubaidah bin Al- Jarrah from Bani Harith bin Fahr (the most trustworthy of the Muslim Nation), Abu Salamah bin 'Abd Al- Asad, Al-Arqam bin Abi Al-Arqam from the tribe of Makhzum, 'Uthman bin Maz'oun and his two brothers Qudama and 'Abdullah, 'Ubaidah bin Al-Harith bin Al-Muttalib bin 'Abd Munaf, Sa'id bin Zaid Al-'Adawi and his wife Fatimah - daughter of Al-Khattab (the sister of 'Umar bin Al-Khattab), Khabbab bin Al- Aratt, 'Abdullâh bin Mas'ud Al-Hadhali and many others. These were the Muslim predecessors. They belonged to various septs of Quraish. Ibn Hisham, a biographer, counted them to be more than forty.

Ibn Ishaq said: "Then people entered the fold of Islam in hosts, men or women and the new faith could no longer be kept secret." The Prophet (Peace be upon him) used to meet and teach, the new converts, the religion in privacy because the call to Islam was still running on an individual and secret basis. Revelation accelerated and continued after the first verses of "O you wrapped in garments." The verses and pieces of Sûrah (chapters) revealed at this time were short ones with wonderful strong pauses and quite fascinating rhythms in full harmony with that delicate whispering setting. The central topic running through them focused on sanctifying the soul, and deterring the Muslims from falling prey to the deceptive glamour of life. The early verses used as well to give a highly accurate account of the Hell and the Garden (Paradise), leading the believers down a new course diametrically opposed to the ill practices rampant amongst their compatriots.

AS-SALAT (the Prayer):

Muqatil bin Sulaiman said: "Salât (prayer) was established as an obligatory ritual at an early stage of the Islamic Call, a two rak'ah (unit of prayer) Salât in the morning and the same in the evening;

"And glorify the praises of your Lord in the 'Ashi (i.e. the time period after the mid-noon till sunset) and in the Ibkar (i.e. the time period from early morning or sunrise till before mid-noon)." [40:55]

$$\text{فَٱصْبِرْ إِنَّ وَعْدَ ٱللَّهِ حَقٌّ وَٱسْتَغْفِرْ لِذَنۢبِكَ وَسَبِّحْ بِحَمْدِ رَبِّكَ بِٱلْعَشِيِّ وَٱلْإِبْكَٰرِ ۝}$$

Ibn Hijr said: "Definitely the Prophet (Peace be upon him) used to pray before 'The Night Journey' but it still remains a matter of controversy whether or not the prayer was established as an obligatory ritual before imposing the rules of the usual five prayers a day. It is related that obligatory prayer was established twice a day, in the morning before sunrise and after sunset. It is reported through a chain of narrators that when the Prophet (Peace be upon him) received the first Revelation, Gabriel - the angel, proceeded and taught him how to observe Wudu (ablution). When the Prophet (Peace be upon him) had finished, he took a handful of water and sprinkled it on his loins.

Ibn Hisham reported that when it was time for prayers, the Messenger of Allâh (Peace be upon him) and his Companions went into a mountain valley to pray secretly. Abu Talib once saw the Messenger of Allâh (Peace be upon him) and Ali praying, he asked them what they were up to. When he got to know that it was obligatory prayer, he told them to stay constant in their practice.

THE QURAISHITES LEARN ABOUT THE CALL:

This stage of the Call, even though conducted in a clandestine manner and on an individual basis, its news leaked out and assumed a public interest all over Makkah. In the beginning, the Makkan leaders did not care much about Muhammad (Peace be upon him) and took no heed of his teachings. At first, they thought that Muhammad (Peace be upon him) was merely a religious philosophist like Omaiyah bin Abi As-Salt, Quss bin Sa'idah, 'Amr bin Nufail and their ilk who used to philosophize on godship and religious obligations. But this attitude of indifference soon changed into real apprehension. The polytheists of Quraish began to watch Muhammad's movements closely and anxiously for fear of spreading his Call and producing a change in the prevalent mentality.

For three underground years of activism, a group of believers emerged stamped by a spirit of fraternity and cooperation with one definite objective in their mind: propagating and deeply establishing the call unto Islam. For full three years Muhammad (Peace be upon him) had been content to teach within a rather narrow circle. The time had, however, come to preach the faith of the Lord openly. The angel Gabriel had brought him down a further Revelation of Allâh's Will to confront his people, invalidate their falsehood and crush down their idolatrous practices.

THE SECOND PHASE OPEN PREACHING - FIRST REVELATION REGARDING REVELATION THE PREACHING:

"And warn your tribe [O Muhammad (Peace be upon him)] of near kindred." [26:214].

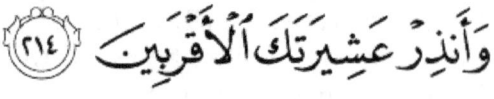

This was the first verse to be revealed in this concern. It is included in Sûrah Ash-Shu'arâ (Chapter 26 - The Poets) which relates the story of Moses (Peace be upon him) from his early days of Prophethood going through his migration with the Children of Israel, their escape from the Pharaoh and his folk, and the drowning Pharaoh and his hosts.

This Chapter in fact narrates the different stages that Moses (Peace be upon him) passed through in his struggle with Pharaoh and the mission of calling his people unto Allâh. Moreover, it includes stories that speak about the terrible end in store for those who belied the Messengers such as the people of Noah, 'Ad, Thamud, Abraham, Lout and Ahlul-Aikah (Companions of the Wood). (A group of people who used to worship a tree called Aikah)

Chronologically, this Chapter belongs to the middle Makkan period, when the contact of the light of Prophecy with the cultural milieu of pagan Makkah was testing the Makkans in their most arrogant mood. The Message that this Chapter communicates is in brief: "The Truth is insurmountable. When the spirit of Prophecy came to Makkah, it was resisted by the votaries of evil; but Truth, unlike falsehood, is bound to stay, whereas falsehood is surely perishable."

CALLING THE CLOSET KINSPEOPLE:

In obedience to Allâh's Commands, Muhammad (Peace be upon him) rallied his kinsmen of Bani Hashim with a group of Bani Al-Muttalib bin 'Abd Munaf. The audience counted forty-five men. Abu Lahab immediately took the initiative and addressed the Prophet (Peace be upon him): "These are your uncles and cousins, speak on to the point, but first of all you have got to know that your kinspeople are not in a position to withstand all the Arabs. Another point you have got to bear in mind is that your relatives are sufficient unto you. If you follow their tradition, it will be easier for them than to face the other clans of Quraish supported by the other Arabs. Verily, I have never heard of anyone who has incurred more harm on his kinspeople than you."

The Messenger of Allâh (Peace be upon him) kept silent and said nothing 7in that meeting. He invited them to another meeting and managed to secure audience. He then stood up and delivered a short speech explaining quite cogently what was at stake. He said: "I celebrate Allâh's praise, I seek His help, I believe in Him, I put my trust in Him, I bear witness that there is no god to be worshipped but Allâh with no associate. A guide can never lie to his people. I swear by Allâh, there is no god but He. I have been sent as a Messenger to you, in particular and to all the people, in general.

I swear by Allâh you will die just as you sleep, you will be resurrected just as you wake up. You will be called to account for your deeds. It is then either Hell forever or the Garden (Paradise) forever."

Abu Talib replied: "We love to help you, accept your advice and believe in your words. These are your kinspeople whom you have collected and I am one of them but I am the fastest to do what you like. Do what you have been ordered. I shall protect and defend you, but I can't quit the religion of 'Abdul-Muttalib."

Abu Lahab then said to Abu Talib:" I swear by Allâh that this is a bad thing. You must stop him before the others do." Abu Talib, however, answered: "I swear by Allâh to protect him as long as I am alive."

ON MOUNT AS-SAFA: After the Messenger of Allâh (Peace be upon him) became sure of Abu Talib's commitment to his protection while he called the people unto Allâh, he stood up on Mount As-Safa one day and called out loudly: "O Sabahah! * "Septs of Quraish came to him. He called them to testify to the Oneness of Allâh and believe in his Messengership and the Day of Resurrection. Al-Bukhari reported part of this story on the authority of Ibn 'Abbas May Allah be pleased with him). He said: "When the following verses were revealed:

"And warn your tribe [O Muhammad (Peace be upon him)] of near kindred." [26:214]

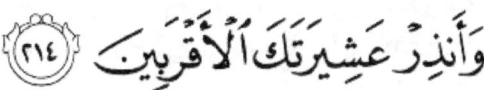

The Messenger of Allâh (Peace be upon him) ascended Mount As-Safa and started to call: "O Bani Fahr! O Bani 'Adi (two septs of Quraish)." Many people gathered and those who couldn't, sent somebody to report to them. Abu Lahab was also present. The Prophet (Peace be upon him) said: "You see, if I were to tell you that there were some horsemen in the valley planning to raid you, will you believe me?" They said: "Yes, we have never experienced any lie from you." He said: "I am a warner to you before a severe torment." Abu Lahab promptly replied: "Perish you all the day! Have you summoned us for such a thing?" The verses were immediately revealed on that occasion:

"Perish the two hands of Abi Lahab..." [111:1].

Muslim reported another part of this story on the authority of Abu Hurairah (May Alah be pleased with him) — He said: "When the following verses were revealed: "And warn your tribe [O Muhammad (Peace be upon him)] of near kindred." [26:214]

The Messenger of Allâh (Peace be upon him) called all the people of Quraish; so they gathered and he gave them a general warning. Then he made a particular reference to certain tribes, and said: "O Quraish, rescue yourselves from the Fire; O people of Bani Ka'b, rescue yourselves from Fire; O Fatimah, daughter of Muhammad (Peace be upon him), rescue yourself from the Fire, for I have no power to protect you from Allâh in anything except that I would sustain relationship with you."

It was verily a loud suggestive Call stating unequivocally to the closest people that belief in his Message constituted the corner-stone of any future relation between him and them, and that the blood-relation on which the whole Arabian life was based, had ceased to exist in the light of that Divine ultimatum.

SHOUTING THE TRUTH AND THE POLYTHEISTS' REACTION:

The Prophet's voice kept reverberating in Makkah until the following verse was revealed: "Therefore proclaim openly (Allâh's Message — Islamic Monotheism), that which you are commanded, and turn away from Al-Mushrikûn (polytheists)." [15:94]

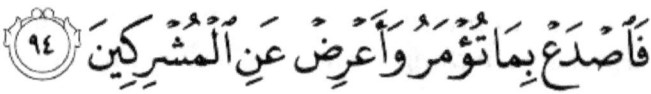

He then commenced discrediting the superstitious practices of idolatry, revealing its worthless reality and utter impotence, and giving concrete proofs that idolatry per se or taking it as the media through which an idolater could come in contact with Allâh, is manifest falsehood.

The Makkans, on their part, burst into outrage and disapproval. Muhammad's (Peace be upon him) words created a thunderbolt that turned the Makkan time-honoured ideological life upside down. They could ill afford to hear someone attaching to polytheists and idolaters, the description of straying people. They started to rally their resources to settle down the affair, quell the onward marching revolution and deal a pre-emptive strike to its votaries before it devours and crushes down their consecrated traditions and long standing heritage. The Makkans had the deep conviction that denying godship to anyone save Allâh and that belief in the Divine Message and the Hereafter are interpreted in terms of complete compliance and absolute commitment, and this in turn leaves no area at all for them to claim authority over themselves and over their wealth, let alone their subordinates.

In short, their arrogated religiously-based supremacy and highhandedness would no longer be in effect; their pleasures would be subordinated to the pleasures of Allâh and His Messenger and lastly they would have to abstain from incurring injustices on those whom they falsely deemed to be weak, and perpetrating dreadful sins in their everyday life. They had already been fully aware of these meanings that is why their souls would not condescend to accept this 'disgraceful' position not out of motives based on dignity and honour but rather because:

"Nay! (Man denies Resurrection and Reckoning. So) he desires to continue committing sins." [75:5]

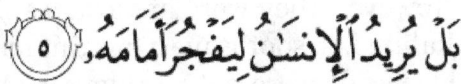

They had been aware of all these consequences but they could afford to do nothing before an honest truthful man who was the highest example of good manners and human values. They had never known such an example in the history of their folks or grandfathers. What would they do? They were baffled, and they had the right to be so.

Following careful deliberations, they hit upon the only target available, i.e. to contact the Messenger's uncle, Abu Talib and request him to intervene and advise his nephew to stop his activities. In order to attach a serious and earnest stamp to their demand, they chose to touch the most sensitive area in Arabian life, viz., ancestral pride. They addressed Abu Talib in the following manner: "O Abu Talib! Your nephew curses our gods; finds faults with our way of life, mocks at our religion and degrades our forefathers; either you must stop him, or you must let us get at him. For you are in the same opposition as we are in opposition to him; and we will rid you of him." Abu Talib tried to appease their wrath by giving them a polite reply. The Prophet (Peace be upon him), however, continued on his way preaching Allâh's religion and calling men hitherto, heedless of all their desperate attempts and malicious intentions

AN ADVISORY COUNCIL TO DEBAR PILGRIMS FROM MUHAMMAD'S CALL:

During those days, Quraish had another serious concern; the proclamation of the Call had only been a few months old when the season of pilgrimage was soon to come. Quraish knew that the Arab delegates were coming within a short time. They agreed that it was necessary to contemplate a device that was bound to alienate the Arab pilgrims from the new faith preached by Muhammad (Peace be upon him). They went to see Al-Waleed bin Al-Mugheerah to deliberate on this issue. Al-Waleed invited them to agree on a unanimous resolution that could enjoy the approbation of them all. However, they were at variance. Some suggested that they describe him as Kahin, i.e., soothsayer; but this suggestion was turned down on grounds that his words were not so rhymed. Others proposed Majnun, i.e., possessed by jinn; this was also rejected because no insinuations peculiar to that state of mind ware detected, they claimed. "Why not say he is a poet?" Some said. Here again they could not reach a common consent, alleging that his words were totally outside the lexicon of poetry. "OK then; let us accuse him of practising witchcraft," was a fourth suggestion.

Here also Al-Waleed showed some reluctance saying that the Prophet (Peace be upon him) was known to have never involved himself in the practice of blowing on the knots, and admitted that his speech was sweet tasting root and branch. He, however, found that the most plausible charge to be levelled against Muhammad (Peace be upon him) was witchcraft. The ungodly company adopted this opinion and agreed to propagate one uniform formula to the effect that he was a magician so powerful and commanding in his art that he would successfully alienate son from father, man from his brother, wife from her husband and man from his clan.

It is noteworthy in this regard to say that Allâh revealed sixteen verses as regards Al-Waleed and the cunning method he contemplated to manipulate the people expected to arrive in Makkah for pilgrimage. Allâh says:

"Verily, he thought and plotted; so let him be cursed! How he plotted! And once more let him be cursed, how he plotted! Then he thought; then he frowned and he looked in a bad tempered way; then he turned back and was proud; then he said: 'This is nothing but magic from that of old; this is nothing but the word of a human being!' " [74:18-25]

إِنَّهُ فَكَّرَ وَقَدَّرَ ﴿١٨﴾

فَقُتِلَ كَيْفَ قَدَّرَ ﴿١٩﴾

ثُمَّ قُتِلَ كَيْفَ قَدَّرَ ﴿٢٠﴾

ثُمَّ نَظَرَ ﴿٢١﴾

ثُمَّ عَبَسَ وَبَسَرَ ﴿٢٢﴾

ثُمَّ أَدْبَرَ وَاسْتَكْبَرَ ﴿٢٣﴾

فَقَالَ إِنْ هَذَا إِلَّا سِحْرٌ يُؤْثَرُ ﴿٢٤﴾

إِنْ هَذَا إِلَّا قَوْلُ الْبَشَرِ ﴿٢٥﴾

The most wicked of them was the sworn enemy of Islam and Muhammad (Peace be upon him), Abu Lahab, who would shadow the Prophet's steps crying aloud, "O men, do not listen to him for he is a liar; he is an apostate." Nevertheless, Muhammad (Peace be upon him) managed to create a stir in the whole area, and even to convince a few people to accept his Call.

THE FIRST MIGRATION TO ABYSSINIA (ETHIOPIA):

The series of persecutions started late in the fourth year of Prophethood, slowly at first, but steadily accelerated and worsened day by day and month by month until the situation got so extremely grave and no longer tolerable in the middle of the fifth year, that the Muslims began to seriously think of feasible ways liable to avert the painful tortures meted out to them.

It was at that gloomy and desperate time that Sûrah Al-Kahf (Chapter 18 — The Cave) was revealed comprising definite answers to the questions with which the polytheists of Makkah constantly pestered the Prophet (Peace be upon him). It comprises three stories that include highly suggestive parables for the true believers to assimilate. The story of the Companions of the Cave implies implicit guidance for the believers to evacuate the hot spots of disbelief and aggression pregnant with the peril of enticement away from the true religion:

The young men said to one another): And when you withdraw from them, and that which they worship, except Allâh, then seek refuge in the Cave, your Lord will open a way for you from His Mercy and will make easy for you your affair (i.e. will give you what you will need of provision, dwelling, etc.) [18:16].

$$\text{وَإِذِ اعْتَزَلْتُمُوهُمْ وَمَا يَعْبُدُونَ إِلَّا اللَّهَ فَأْوُوا إِلَى الْكَهْفِ يَنشُرْ لَكُمْ رَبُّكُم مِّن رَّحْمَتِهِ وَيُهَيِّئْ لَكُم مِّنْ أَمْرِكُم مِّرْفَقًا ﴿١٦﴾}$$

Next, there is the story of Al-Khidr (The Teacher of Arabia) and Moses (Peace be upon him) in a clear and delicate reference to the vicissitudes of life. Future circumstances of life are not necessarily the products of the prevalent conditions, they might be categorically the opposite.

In other words, the war waged against the Muslims would in the future assume a different turn, and the tyrannous oppressors would one day come to suffer and be subjected to the same tortures to which the Muslims were then put. Furthermore, there is the story of Dhul-Qarnain (The Two Horned One), the powerful ruler of west and east. This story says explicitly that Allâh takes His righteous servants to inherit the earth and whatever in it. It also speaks that Allâh raises a righteous man every now and then to protect the weak against the strong.

Sûrah Az-Zumar (Chapter 39 — The Crowds) was then revealed pointing directly to migration and stating that the earth is spacious enough and the believers must not consider themselves constrained by the forces of tyranny and evil: "Good is (the reward) for those who do good in this world, and Allâh's earth is spacious (so if you cannot worship Allâh at a place, then go to another)! Only those who are patient shall receive their rewards in full without reckoning." [39:10].

قُلْ يَٰعِبَادِ ٱلَّذِينَ ءَامَنُواْ ٱتَّقُواْ رَبَّكُمْ لِلَّذِينَ أَحْسَنُواْ فِى هَٰذِهِ ٱلدُّنْيَا حَسَنَةٌ وَأَرْضُ ٱللَّهِ وَٰسِعَةٌ إِنَّمَا يُوَفَّى ٱلصَّٰبِرُونَ أَجْرَهُم بِغَيْرِ حِسَابٍ ۝

The Prophet (Peace be upon him) had already known that Ashamah Negus, king of Abyssinia (Ethiopia), was a fair ruler who would not wrong any of his subordinates, so he permitted some of his followers to seek asylum there in Abyssinia (Ethiopia).

In Rajab of the fifth year of Prophethood, a group of twelve men and four women left for Abyssinia (Ethiopia). Among the emigrants were 'Uthman bin 'Affan and his wife Ruqaiyah [the daughter of the Prophet (Peace be upon him)]. With respect to these two emigrants, the Prophet (Peace be upon him) said: "They are the first people to migrate in the cause of Allâh after Abraham and Lot (Peace be upon them)."

They sneaked out of Makkah under the heavy curtain of a dark night and headed for the sea where two boats happened to be sailing for Abyssinia (Ethiopia), their destination. News of their intended departure reached the ears of Quraish, so some men were despatched in their pursuit, but the believers had already left Shuaibah Port towards their secure haven where they were received warmly and accorded due hospitality.

In Ramadan of the same year, the Prophet (Peace be upon him) went into the Holy Sanctuary where there was a large host of Quraish polytheists, including some notables and celebrities. Suddenly he began reciting Sûrah An-Najm (Chapter 41 — The Star). The awe-inspiring Words of Allâh descended unawares upon them and they immediately got stunned by them. It was the first time for them to be shocked by the truthful Revelation. It had formerly been the favourite trick of those people who wished to dishonour Revelation, not only not to listen to it themselves but also to talk loudly and insolently when it was being read, so that even the true listeners may not be able to hear. They used to think that they were drowning the Voice of Allâh; in fact, they were piling up misery for themselves, for Allâh's Voice can never be silenced, "And those who disbelieve say: "Listen not to this Qur'ân, and make noise in the midst of its (recitation) that you may overcome." [41:26].

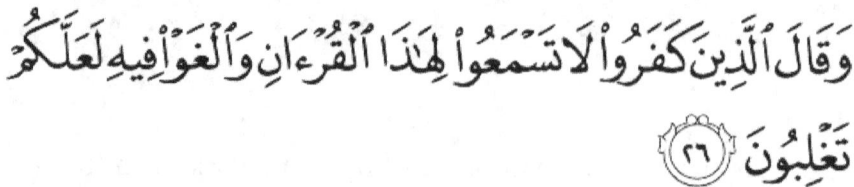

When the unspeakably fascinating Words of Allâh came into direct contact with their hearts, they were entranced and got oblivious of the materialistic world around them and were caught in a state of full attentiveness to the Divine Words to such an extent that when the Prophet (Peace be upon him) reached the stormy heart-beating ending: "So fall you down in prostration to Allâh and worship Him (Alone)." [53:62]

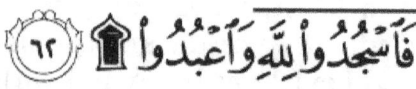

The idolaters, unconsciously and with full compliance, prostrated themselves in absolute god-fearing and stainless devotion. It was in fact the wonderful moment of the Truth that cleaved through the obdurate souls of the haughty and the attitude of the scoffers. They stood aghast when they perceived that Allâh's Words had conquered their hearts and done the same thing that they had been trying hard to annihilate and exterminate. Their co-polytheists who had not been present on the scene reproached and blamed them severely; consequently they began to fabricate lies and calumniate the Prophet (Peace be upon him) alleging that he had attached to their idols great veneration and ascribed to them the power of desirable intercession. All of these were desperate attempts made to establish an excusable justification for their prostrating themselves with the Prophet (Peace be upon him) on that day. Of course, this foolish and iniquitous slanderous behaviour was in line with their life-consecrated practice of telling lies and plot hatching.

News of this incident was misreported to the Muslim emigrants in Abyssinia (Ethiopia). They were informed that the whole of Quraish had embraced Islam so they made their way back home. They arrived in Makkah in Shawwal of the same year. When they were only an hour's travel from Makkah, the reality of the situation was discovered. Some of them returned to Abyssinia (Ethiopia), others sneaked secretly into the city or went in publicly but under the tutelage of a local notable. However, due to the news that transpired to the Makkans about the good hospitality and warm welcome that the Muslims were accorded in Abyssinia (Ethiopia), the polytheists got terribly indignant and started to mete out severer and more horrible maltreatment andtortures to the Muslims. Thereupon the Messenger of Allâh (Peace be upon him) deemed it imperative to permit the helpless creatures to seek asylum in Abyssinia (Ethiopia) for the second time. Migration this time was not as easy as it was the previous time, for Quraish was on the alert to the least suspicious moves of the Muslims. In due course, however, the Muslims managed their affairs too fast for the Quraishites to thwart their attempt of escape. The group of emigrants this time comprised eighty three men and nineteen or, in some versions, eighteen women. Whether or not 'Ammar was included is still a matter of doubt.

QURAISH'S MACHINATION AGAINSTN THE EMIGRANTS:

Quraish could not tolerate the prospect of a secure haven available for the Muslims in Abyssinia (Ethiopia), so they despatched two staunch envoys to demand their extradition. They were 'Amr bin Al-'As and 'Abdullah bin Abi Rabi'a — before embracing Islam. They had taken with them valuable gifts to the king and his clergy, and had been able to win some of the courtiers over to their side. The pagan envoys claimed that the Muslim refugees should be expelled from Abyssinia (Ethiopia) and made over to them, on the ground that they had abandoned the religion of their forefathers, and their leader was preaching a religion different from theirs and from that of the king.

The king summoned the Muslims to the court and asked them to explain the teachings of their religion. The Muslim emigrants had decided to tell the whole truth whatever the consequences were. Ja'far bin Abi Talib stood up and addressed the king in the following words: "O king! we were plunged in the depth of ignorance and barbarism; we adored idols, we lived in unchastity, we ate the dead bodies, and we spoke abominations, we disregarded every feeling of humanity, and the duties of hospitality and neighbourhood were neglected; we knew no law but that of the strong, when Allâh raised among us a man, of whose birth, truthfulness, honesty, and purity we were aware; and he called to the Oneness of Allâh, and taught us not to associate anything with Him. He forbade us the worship of idols; and he enjoined us to speak the truth, to be faithful to our trusts, to be merciful and to regard the rights of the neighbours and kith and kin; he forbade us to speak evil of women, or to eat the substance of orphans; he ordered us to fly from the vices, and to abstain from evil; to offer prayers, to render alms, and to observe fast. We have believed in him, we have accepted his teachings and his injunctions to worship Allâh, and not to associate anything with Him, and we have allowed what He has allowed, and prohibited what He has prohibited. For this reason, our people have risen against us, have persecuted us in order to make us forsake the worship of Allâh and return to the worship of idols and other abominations. They have tortured and injured us, until finding no safety among them, we have come to your country, and hope you will protect us from oppression."

The king was very much impressed by these words and asked the Muslims to recite some of Allâh's Revelation. Ja'far recited the opening verses of Sûrah Maryam (Chapter 19 — Mary) wherein is told the story of the birth of both John and Jesus Christ, down to the account of Mary having been fed with the food miraculously. Thereupon the king, along with the bishops of his realm, was moved to tears that rolled down his cheeks and even wet his beard. Here, the Negus exclaimed: "It seems as if these words and those which were revealed to Jesus are the rays of the light which have radiated from the same source." Turning to the crest-fallen envoys of Quraish, he said, "I am afraid, I cannot give you back these refugees. They are free to live and worship in my realm as they please."

On the morrow, the two envoys again went to the king and said that Muhammad (Peace be upon him) and his followers blasphemed Jesus Christ. Again the Muslims were summoned and asked what they thought of Jesus. Ja'far again stood up and replied: "We speak about Jesus as we have been taught by our Prophet (Peace be upon him), that is, he is the servant of Allâh, His Messenger, His spirit and His Word breathed into Virgin Mary." The king at once remarked, "Even so do we believe. Blessed be you, and blessed be your master." Then turning to the frowning envoys and to his bishops who got angry, he said: "You may fret and fume as you like but Jesus is nothing more than what Ja'far has said about him." He then assured the Muslims of full protection. He returned to the envoys of Quraish, the gifts they had brought with them and sent them away. The Muslims lived in Abyssinia (Ethiopia) unmolested for a number of years till they returned to Madinah.

In this way Quraish's malicious intentions recoiled on them and their machination met with utter failure. They came to fully realize that the grudge they nursed against the Muslims would not operate but within their realm of Makkah. They consequently began to entertain a horrible idea of silencing the advocate of the new Call once and for all, through various channels of brutality, or else killing him. An obstinate difficulty, however, used to curtail any move in this direction embodied by the Prophet's uncle Abu Talib and the powerful social standing he used to enjoy as well as the full protection and support he used to lend to his nephew.

The pagans of Makkah therefore decided to approach Abu Talib for the second time and insisted that he put a stop to his nephew's activities, which if allowed unchecked, they said, would involve him into severe hostility. Abu Talib was deeply distressed at this open threat and the breach with his people and their enmity, but he could not afford to desert the Messenger too. He sent for his nephew and told him what the people had said, "Spare me and yourself and put not burden on me that I can't bear." Upon this the Prophet (Peace be upon him) thought that his uncle would let him down and would no longer support him, so he replied: "O my uncle! By Allâh if they put the sun in my right hand and the moon in my left on condition that I abandon this course, until Allâh has made me victorious, or I perish therein, I would not abandon it." The Prophet (Peace be upon him) got up, and as he turned away, his uncle called him and said, "Come back, my nephew," and when he came back, he said, "Go and preach what you please, for by Allâh I will never forsake you."

He then recited two lines of verse pregnant with meanings of full support to the Prophet (Peace be upon him) and absolute gratification by the course that his nephew had chalked out in Arabia.

ONCE MORE QURAISH APPROACHES ABU TALIB:

Quraish, seeing that the Messenger of Allâh (Peace be upon him) was still intent on his Call, realized that Abu Talib would never forsake his nephew even if this incurred their enmity. Some of them then went to see him once more taking with them a youth called 'Amarah bin Al-Waleed bin Al-Mugheerah, and said, "O Abu Talib!

We have brought you a smart boy still in the bloom of his youth, to make use of his mind and strength and take him as your son in exchange for your nephew, who has run counter to your religion, brought about social discord, found fault with your way of life, so that we kill him and rid you of his endless troubles; just man for man." Abu Talib's reply was, "It is really an unfair bargain.

You give me your son to bring him up and I give you my son to kill him! By Allâh, it is something incredible!!" Al-Mut'im bin 'Adi, a member of the delegation, interrupted saying that Quraish had been fair in that bargain because "they meant only to rid you of that source of hateful trouble, but as I see you are determined to refuse their favours." Abu Talib, of course, turned down all their offers and challenged them to do whatever they pleased. Historical resources do not give the exact date of these two meetings with Abu Talib. They, however, seem more likely to have taken place in the sixth year of Prophethood with a brief lapse of time in between.

THE TYRANTS' DECISION TO KILL THE PROPHET:

Now that all the schemes of Quraish had failed, they resorted to their old practices of persecution and inflicting tortures on the Muslims in a more serious and brutal manner than ever before. They also began to nurse the idea of killing the Prophet (Peace be upon him). In fact, contrary to their expectations, this new method and this very idea served indirectly to consolidate the Call to Islam and support it with the conversion of two staunch and mighty heroes of Makkah, i.e. Hamzah bin 'Abdul-Muttalib and 'Umar bin Al-Khattab (May Allah be pleased with him).

'Utaibah bin Abi Lahab once approached the Prophet (Peace be upon him) and most defiantly and brazenly shouted at him, "I disbelieve in: "By the star when it goes down." [53:1] and in "Then he (Gabriel) approached and came closer." [53:8] In other words: "I do not believe in any of the Qur'ân." He then started to deal highhandedly with Muhammad (Peace be upon him) and laid violent hand on him, tore his shirt and spat into his face but his saliva missed the Holy face of the Prophet (Peace be upon him). Thereupon, the Prophet (Peace be upon him) invoked Allâh's wrath on 'Utaibah and supplicated: "O Allâh! Set one of Your dogs on him."

Allâh responded positively to Muhammad's supplication, and it happened in the following manner: Once 'Utaibah with some of his compatriots from Quraish set out for Syria and took accommodation in Az-Zarqa'.

There a lion approached the group to the great fear of 'Utbah, who at once recalled Muhammad's words in supplication, and said: "Woe to my brother! This lion will surely devour me just as Muhammad (Peace be upon him) supplicated. He has really killed me in Syria while he is in Makkah." The lion did really rush like lightning, snatched 'Utbah from amongst his people and crushed his head.

It is also reported that a wretched idolater from Quraish, named 'Uqbah bin 'Abi Mu'ait once trod on the Prophet's neck while he was prostrating himself in prayer until his eyes protruded.

More details reported by Ibn Ishaq testify to the tyrants' deeply-established intentions of killing the Prophet (Peace be upon him). Abu Jahl, the archenemy of Islam, once addressed some of his accomplices: "O people of Quraish! It seems that Muhammad (Peace be upon him) is determined to go on finding fault with our religion, degrading our forefathers, discrediting our way of life and abusing our gods. I bear witness to our god that I will carry a too heavy rock and drop it on Muhammad's head while he is in prostration to rid you of him, once and for all. I am not afraid of whatever his sept, Banu 'Abd Munaf, might do." The terrible unfortunate audience endorsed his plan and encouraged him to translate it into a decisive deed.

In the morning of the following day, Abu Jahl lay waiting for the arrival of the Messenger of Allâh (Peace be upon him) to offer prayer. The people of Quraish were in their assembly rooms waiting for news. When the Prophet (Peace be upon him) prostrated himself, Abu Jahl proceeded carrying the big rock to fulfill his wicked intention. No sooner had he approached closer to the Prophet (Peace be upon him) than he withdraw pale-faced, shuddering with his hands strained the rock falling off. Thereupon, the people watching hurried forward asking him what the matter was. He replied: "When I approached, a male-camel unusual in figure with fearful canines intercepted and almost devoured me."

Ibn Ishaq reported that the Prophet (Peace be upon him), in the context of his comment on the incident, said "It was Gabriel (Peace be upon him), if Abu Jahl had approached closer, he would have killed him." Even so the tyrants of Quraish would not be admonished, contrariwise, the idea of killing the Prophet (Peace be upon him) was still being nourished in their iniquitous hearts. On the authority of 'Abdullah bin 'Amr bin Al-'As, some people of Quraish were in a place called Al-Hijr complaining that they had been too patient with the Prophet (Peace be upon him), who suddenly appeared and began his usual circumambulation. They started to wink at him and utter sarcastic remarks but he remained silent for two times, then on the third, he stopped and addressed the infidels saying:

"O people of Quraish! Hearken, I swear by Allâh in Whose Hand is my soul, that you will one day be slaughtered to pieces." As soon as the Prophet (Peace be upon him) uttered his word of slaughter, they all stood aghast and switched off to a new style of language smacking of fear and even horror trying to soothe his anger and comfort him saying: "You can leave Abul Qasim, for you have never been foolish."

'Urwa bin Az-Zubair narrated: I asked Abdullah bin 'Amr bin Al-'As to tell me of the worst thing that the pagans did to the Prophet (Peace be upon him). He said: "While the Prophet (Peace be upon him) was praying in Al-Hijr of Al-Ka'bah, 'Uqbah bin Al-Mu'ait came and put his garment around the Prophet's neck and throttled him violently. Abu Bakr came and caught him by his shoulder and pushed him away from the Prophet (Peace be upon him) and said: "Do you want to kill a man just because he says, My Lord is Allâh?"

THE CONVERSION OF HAMZAH BIN 'ABDUL-MUTTALIB: In a gloomy atmosphere infested with dark clouds of iniquity and tyranny, there shone on the horizon a promising light for the oppressed, i.e. the conversion of Hamzah bin 'Abdul-Muttalib in Dhul Hijjah, the sixth year of Prophethood. It is recorded that the Prophet (Peace be upon him) was one day seated on the hillock of Safa when Abu Jahl happened to pass by and accused the religion preached by him.

Muhammad (Peace be upon him), however, kept silent and did not utter a single word. Abu Jahl went on unchecked, took a stone and cracked the Prophet's head which began to bleed. The aggressor then went to join the Quraishites in their assembly place. It so happened that shortly after that, Hamzah, while returning from a hunting expedition, passed by the same way, his bow hanging by his shoulder. A slave-girl belonging to 'Abdullah bin Jada'an, who had noted the impertinence of Abu Jahl, told him the whole story of the attack on the Prophet (Peace be upon him). On hearing that, Hamzah was deeply offended and hurried to Al-Ka'bah and there, in the courtyard of the Holy Sanctuary, found Abu Jahl sitting with a company of Quraishites. Hamzah rushed upon him and struck his bow upon his head violently and said: "Ah! You have been abusing Muhammad (Peace be upon him); I too follow his religion and profess what he preaches." The men of Bani Makhzum came to his help, and men of Bani Hashim wanted to render help, but Abu Jahl sent them away saying: "Let Abu 'Ummarah alone, by Allâh I did revile his nephew shamelessly." In fact, Hamzah's conversion derived initially from the pride of a man who would not accept the notion of others humiliating his relative. Later on, however, Allâh purified his nature and he managed to grasp the most trustworthy hand-hold (Faith in Allâh). He proved to be a source of great strength to the Islamic Faith and its followers.

THE CONVERSION OF 'UMAR BIN AL-KHATTAB:

Another significant addition to the strength of Islam was the conversion of 'Umar bin Al-Khattab in Dhul-Hijjah, the sixth year of Prophethood, three days following the conversion of Hamzah.] He was a man of dauntless courage and resolution, feared and respected in Makkah, and hitherto a bitter opponent of the new religion. The traditional account reveals that the Prophet (Peace be upon him) once raised his hands in prayer and said: "O Allâh! Give strength to Islam especially through either of two men you love more: 'Umar bin Al- Khattab or Abu Jahl bin Hisham." 'Umar, obviously, was the one who merited that privilege.

When we scrutinize the several versions that speak of 'Umar's conversion, we can safely conclude that various contradictory emotions used to conflict with one another within his soul. On the one hand, he used to highly regard the traditions of his people, and was habituated to the practice of indulgence in wine orgies; on the other hand, he greatly admired the stamina of the Muslims and their relentless dedication to their faith. These two extreme views created a sort of skepticism in himind and made him at times tend to believe that the doctrines of Islam could bear better and more sacred seeds of life that is why he would always experience fits of outrage directly followed by unexpected enervation. On the whole, the account of his conversion is very interesting and requires us to go into some details.

One day, 'Umar bin Al-Khattab set out from his house, and headed for the Holy Sanctuary where he saw the Prophet (Peace be upon him) offering prayer and overheard him reciting the Sûrah Al-Hâqqah (Chapter 69 — The Reality) of the Noble Qur'ân. The Words of Allâh appealed to him and touched the innermost cells of his heart. He felt that they derived from unusual composition, and he began to question his people's allegations as regards the man-composed poetry or words of a soothsayer that they used to attach to the Noble Qur'ân. The Prophet (Peace be upon him) went on to recite: "That this is verily the word of an honoured Messenger (i.e. Gabriel or Muhammad (Peace be upon him) which he has brought from Allâh). It is not the word of a poet, little is that you believe! Nor is it the word of a soothsayer (or a foreteller), little is that you remember! This is the Revelation sent down from the Lord of the 'Alamin (mankind, jinns and all that exists)." [69:40-43]

إِنَّهُۥ لَقَوْلُ رَسُولٍ كَرِيمٍ ﴿٤٠﴾

وَمَا هُوَ بِقَوْلِ شَاعِرٍ قَلِيلًا مَّا تُؤْمِنُونَ ﴿٤١﴾

وَلَا بِقَوْلِ كَاهِنٍ قَلِيلًا مَّا تَذَكَّرُونَ ﴿٤٢﴾

At that very moment, Islam permeated his heart. However, the dark layer of pre-Islamic tendencies, the deep-seated traditional bigotry as well as the blind pride in his forefathers overshadowed the essence of the great Truth that began to feel its way reluctantly into his heart. He, therefore, persisted in his atrocities against Islam and its adherents unmindful of the pure and true-to-man's nature feeling that lay behind that fragile cover of pre-Islamic ignorance and mentality.

His sharp temper and excessive enmity towards the Prophet (Peace be upon him) led him one day to leave his house, sword in hand, with the intention of killing the Prophet (Peace be upon him) . He was in a fit of anger and was fretting and fuming. Nu'aim bin 'Abdullah, a friend of 'Umar's, met him accidentally half way. What had caused so much excitement in him and on whom was the fury to burst, he inquired casually. 'Umar said furiously: "To destroy the man Muhammad (Peace be upon him) this apostate, who has shattered the unity of Quraish, picked holes in their religion, found folly with their wise men and blasphemed their gods." "'Umar, I am sure, your soul has deceived you, do you think that Banu 'Abd Munaf would let you walk on earth if you slain Muhammad (Peace be upon him)? Why don't you take care of your own family first and set them right?"

"Which of the folk of my house?" asked 'Umar angrily. "Your brother-in-law and your sister have apostatized [meaning to say: They have become followers of Muhammad (Peace be upon him)] and abandoned your religion." 'Umar directed his footsteps to his sister's house. As he drew near, he heard the voice of Khabbab bin Aratt, who was reading the Qur'ânic Chapter Tâ-Hâ (mystic letters, T. H.) to both of them. Khabbab, perceiving the noise of his footsteps retired to a closet. Fatimah, 'Umar's sister, took hold of the leaf and hid it. But 'Umar had already heard the voice. "What sound was that I have heard just now?" shouted the son of Khattab, entering angrily. Both his sister and her husband replied, "You heard nothing." "Nay," said he swearing fiercely, "I have heard that you have apostatized." He plunged forward towards his brother-in-law and beat him severely, but Fatimah rushed to the rescue of her husband. Thereupon, 'Umar fell upon his sister and struck upon her head.

The husband and wife could not contain themselves and cried aloud: "Yes, we are Muslims, we believe in Allâh and His Messenger Muhammad (Peace be upon him) so do what you will." When 'Umar saw the face of his dear sister besmeared with blood, he was softened and said: "Let me see what you were reading, so that I may see what Muhammad (Peace be upon him) has brought." Fatimah was satisfied with the assurance, but said: "O brother, you are unclean on account of your idolatry, none but the pure may touch it. So go and wash first." He did so, and took the page and read the opening verses of the Chapter Tâ-Hâ until he reached: "Verily! I am Allâh! Lâ ilâha illa Ana (none has the right to be worshipped but I), so worship Me and offer prayers perfectly (Iqâmat-as-Salât), for My Remembrance." [20:14].

إِنَّنِي أَنَا ٱللَّهُ لَآ إِلَٰهَ إِلَّآ أَنَا۠ فَٱعْبُدْنِي وَأَقِمِ ٱلصَّلَوٰةَ لِذِكْرِىٓ ﴿١٤﴾

'Umar read the verses with great interest and was much entranced with them. "How excellent it is, and how graceful! Please guide me to Muhammad (Peace be upon him)." said he. And when he heard that, Khabbab came out of concealment and said, "O 'Umar, I hope that Allâh has answered the prayer of the Prophet (Peace be upon him), for I heard him say: 'O Allâh! Strengthen Islam through either 'Umar bin Al-Khattab or Abu Jahl bin Hisham.'" 'Umar then left for a house in Safa where Muhammad (Peace be upon him) had been holding secret meetings along with his Companions. 'Umar reached that place with the sword swinging by his arm. He knocked at the door. The Companions of the Prophet (Peace be upon him) turned to see who the intruder was. One of them peeped through a chink in the door and reeled back exclaiming: "It is 'Umar with his sword." Hamzah, dispelling the fears of his friends, said: "Let him in. As a friend he is welcome. As a foe, he will have his head cut off with his own sword." The Prophet (Peace be upon him) asked his Companions to open the door. In came the son of Khattab. The Prophet (Peace be upon him) advanced to receive the dreadful visitor, caught him by his garment and scabbard, and asked him the reason of his visit. At that 'Umar replied: "O Messenger of Allâh (Peace be upon him), I come to you in order to believe in Allâh and his Messenger and that which he has brought from his Lord." Filled with delight, Muhammad (Peace be upon him) together with his Companions, cried aloud: 'Allâhu Akbar' (Allâh is Great).

The conversion of 'Umar was a real triumph for the cause of Islam. So great and instant was the effect of his conversion on the situation that the believers who had hitherto worshipped Allâh within their four walls in secret now assembled and performed their rites of worship openly in the Holy Sanctuary itself. This raised their spirits, and dread and uneasiness began to seize Quraish.

Ibn Ishaq narrated on the authority of 'Umar (May Allah be pleased), "When I embraced Islam, I remembered the archenemy of Muhammad (Peace be upon him), i.e. Abu Jahl. I set out, and knocked at his door. When he came out to see me, I told him directly that I had embraced Islam. He immediately slammed the door repulsively denouncing my move as infamous and my face as ugly." In fact, 'Umar's conversion created a great deal of stir in Makkah that some people denounced him as an apostate, yet he would never waver in Faith, on the contrary, he persisted in his stance even at the peril of his life. The polytheists of Quraish marched towards his house with the intention of killing him. 'Abdullah bin 'Umar (May Allah be pleased with him) narrated: While 'Umar was at home in a state of fear, there came Al-'As bin Wa'il As-Sahmy Abu 'Amr, wearing an embroidered cloak and a shirt having silk hems. He was from the tribe of Bani Sahm who were our allies during the pre-Islamic period of ignorance. Al-'As said to 'Umar: What's wrong with you? He said: Your people claim that they will kill me if I become a Muslim. Al-'As said: Nobody will harm you after I have given protection to you. So Al-'As went out and met the people streaming in the whole valley. He said: Where are you going? They replied: We want son of Al-Khattab who has embraced Islam. Al-'As said: There is no way for anybody to touch him. So the people retreated.

With respect to the Muslims in Makkah, 'Umar's conversion had a different tremendous impact. Mujahid, on the authority of Ibn Al-'Abbas (May Allah be pleased with him) related that he had asked 'Umar bin Al-Khattab why he had been given the epithet of Al-Farouque (he who distinguishes truth from falsehood), he replied: After I had embraced Islam, I asked the Prophet (Peace be upon him): 'Aren't we on the right path here and Hereafter?'

The Prophet (Peace be upon him) answered: 'Of course you are! I swear by Allâh in Whose Hand my soul is, that you are right in this world and in the hereafter.' I, therefore, asked the Prophet (Peace be upon him) 'Why we then had to conduct clandestine activism. I swear by Allâh Who has sent you with the Truth, that we will leave our concealment and proclaim our noble cause publicly.' We then went out in two groups, Hamzah leading one and I the other. We headed for the Mosque in broad daylight when the polytheists of Quraish saw us, their faces went pale and got incredibly depressed and resentful. On that very occasion, the Prophet (Peace be upon him) attached to me the epithet of Al-Farouque. Ibn Mas'ud (May Allah be pleased with him) related that they (the Muslims) had never been able to observe their religious rites inside the Holy Sanctuary except when 'Umar embraced Islam.

Suhaib bin Sinan (May Allah be pleased with him), in the same context, said that it was only after 'Umar's conversion, that we started to proclaim our Call, assemble around and circumambulate the Sacred House freely. We even dared retaliate against some of the injustices done to harm us. In the same context, Ibn Mas'ud said: We have been strengthened a lot since 'Umar embraced Islam.

QURAISH'S REPRESENTATIVE NEGOTIATES WITH THE MESSENGER OF ALLAH:

Shortly after the conversion of these two powerful heroes, Hamzah bin 'Abdul-Muttalib and 'Umar bin Al-Khattab (May Allah be pleased with him), the clouds of tyranny and oppression started to clear away and the polytheists realized that it was no use meting out torture to the Muslims. They consequently began to direct their campaign to a different course. The authentic records of the biography of the Prophet (Peace be upon him) show that it had occurred to the Makkan leaders to credit Muhammad (Peace be upon him) with ambition. They, therefore, time and again plied him with temptation.

One day some of the important men of Makkah gathered in the enclosure of Al-Ka'bah, and 'Utbah bin Rabi'a, a chief among them, offered to approach the Prophet (Peace be upon him) and contract a bargain with him whereby they give him whatever worldly wealth he asks for, on condition that he keep silent and no longer proclaim his new faith. The people of Quraish endorsed his proposal and requested him to undertake that task. 'Utbah came closer to Muhammad (Peace be upon him) and addressed him in the following words:

We have seen no other man of Arabia, who has brought so great a calamity to a nation, as you have done. You have outraged our gods and religion and taxed our forefathers and wise men with impiety and error and created strife amongst us. You have left no stone unturned to estrange the relations with us. If you are doing all this with a view to getting wealth, we will join together to give you greater riches than any Quraishite has possessed. If ambition moves you, we will make you our chief. If you desire kingship we will readily offer you that. If you are under the power of an evil spirit which seems to haunt and dominate you so that you cannot shake off its yoke, then we shall call in skilful physicians to cure you.

"Have you said all?" asked Muhammad (Peace be upon him); and then hearing that all had been said, he spoke forth, and said: "In the Name of Allâh, the Most Beneficent, the Most Merciful. Hâ-Mîm. [These letters are one of the miracles of the Qur'ân, and none but Allâh (Alone) knows their meanings]. A revelation from Allâh, the Most Beneficent, the Most Merciful. A Book whereof the verses are explained in detail;

— a Qur'ân in Arabic for people who know. Giving glad tidings [of Paradise to the one who believes in the Oneness of Allâh (i.e. Islamic Monotheism) and fears Allâh much (abstains from all kinds of sins and evil deeds.) and loves Allâh much (performing all kinds of good deeds which He has ordained)], and warning (of punishment in the Hell-fire to the one who disbelieves in the Oneness of Allâh), but most of them turn away, so they listen not. And they say: Our hearts are under coverings (screened) from that to which you invite us ..." [41: 1-5]

$$\text{حم ﴿١﴾}$$

$$\text{تَنزِيلٌ مِّنَ ٱلرَّحْمَٰنِ ٱلرَّحِيمِ ﴿٢﴾}$$

$$\text{كِتَابٌ فُصِّلَتْ ءَايَاتُهُ قُرْءَانًا عَرَبِيًّا لِّقَوْمٍ يَعْلَمُونَ ﴿٣﴾}$$

$$\text{بَشِيرًا وَنَذِيرًا فَأَعْرَضَ أَكْثَرُهُمْ فَهُمْ لَا يَسْمَعُونَ ﴿٤﴾}$$

$$\text{وَقَالُوا قُلُوبُنَا فِي أَكِنَّةٍ مِّمَّا تَدْعُونَا إِلَيْهِ وَفِي ءَاذَانِنَا وَقْرٌ وَمِنْ بَيْنِنَا وَبَيْنِكَ حِجَابٌ فَٱعْمَلْ إِنَّنَا عَامِلُونَ ﴿٥﴾}$$

The Messenger of Allâh (Peace be upon him) went on reciting the Chapter while 'Utbah sitting and listening attentively with his hand behind his back to support him. When the Messenger reached the verse that required prostration, he immediately prostrated himself. After that, he turned to 'Utbah saying: "Well Abu Al-Waleed! You have heard my reply, you are now free to do whatever you please." 'Utbah then retired to his company to apprise them of the Prophet's attitude. When his compatriots saw him, they swore that he had returned to them with a countenance unlike the one he had before meeting the Prophet (Peace be upon him). He immediately communicated to them the details of the talk he gave and the reply he received, and appended saying: "I have never heard words similar to those ones he recited. They definitely relate neither to poetry nor to witchcraft nor do they derive from soothsaying. O people of Quraish! I request you to heed my advice and grant the man full freedom to pursue his goals, in which case you could safely detach yourselves from him. I swear that his words bear a supreme Message. Should the other Arabs rid you of him, they will then spare you the trouble, on the other hand if he accedes to power over the Arabs, then you will bask in his kingship and share him his might." These words of course fell on deaf ears, and did not appeal to the infidels, who jeered at 'Utbah and claimed that the Prophet (Peace be upon him) had bewitched him.

In another version of the same event, it is related that 'Utbah went on attentively listening to the Prophet (Peace be upon him) until the latter began to recite Allâh's Words: "But if they turn away, they say [O Muhammad (Peace be upon him)]: "I have warned you of a Sa'iqa (a destructive awful cry, torment, hit, a thunder-bolt) like the Sa'iqa which overtook 'Ad and Thamûd (people)." [41:13]

فَإِنْ أَعْرَضُوا۟ فَقُلْ أَنذَرْتُكُمْ صَٰعِقَةً مِّثْلَ صَٰعِقَةِ عَادٍ وَثَمُودَ ۝

Here 'Utbah stood up panicked and stunned putting his hand on the Prophet's mouth beseeching him: "I beg you in the Name of Allâh and uterine ties to stop lest the calamity should befall the people of Quraish." He then hurriedly returned to his compatriots and informed them of what he had heard.

ABU TALIB ASSEMBLES BANI HASHIM ND BANI AL-MUTTALIB: The new and welcome changes notwithstanding, Abu Talib still had a deep sensation of fear over his nephew. He deliberated on the previous series of incidents including the barter affair of 'Amarah bin Al-Waleed, Abu Jahl's rock, 'Uqbah's attempt to choke the Prophet (Peace be upon him), and finally 'Umar's (before conversion) intention to kill Muhammad (Peace be upon him). The wise man understood that all of these unequivocally smacked of a serious plot being hatched to disregard his status as a custodian of the Prophet (Peace be upon him), and kill the latter publicly. In the event of such a thing, Abu Talib deeply believed, neither 'Umar nor Hamzah would be of any avail, socially powerful though they were.

Abu Talib was right. The polytheists had laid a carefully-studied plan to kill the Prophet (Peace be upon him), and banded together to put their plan into effect. He, therefore, assembled his kinsfolk of Bani Hashim and Bani Al-Muttalib, sons of 'Abd Munaf and exhorted them to immunize and defend his nephew. All of them, whether believers or disbelievers, responded positively except his brother Abu Lahab, who sided with the idolaters.

GENERAL SOCIAL BOYCOTT:

Four events of special significance occurred within less than four weeks — the conversion of Hamzah, the conversion of 'Umar, Muhammad's (Peace be upon him) refusal to negotiate any sort of compromise and then the pact drawn up between Banu Muttalib and Banu Hashim to immunize Muhammad (Peace be upon him) and shield him against any treacherous attempt to kill him. The polytheists were baffled and at a loss as to what course they would follow to rid themselves of this obstinate and relentless obstacle that had appeared to shatter to pieces their whole tradition of life. They had already been aware that if they killed Muhammad (Peace be upon him) the blood would surely flow profusely in the valleys of Makkah and they would certainly be exterminated. Taking this dreadful prospect into consideration, they grudgingly resorted to a different iniquitous course that would not imply murder.

A PACT OF INJUSTICE AND AGGRESSION:

The pagans of Makkah held a meeting in a place called Wadi Al-Muhassab, and formed a confederation hostile to both Bani Hashim and Bani Al-Muttalib. They decided not to have any business dealings with them nor any sort of inter-marriage. Social relations, visits and even verbal contacts with Muhammad (Peace be upon him) and his supporters would discontinue until the Prophet (Peace be upon him) was given up to them to be killed. The articles of their proclamation, which had provided for merciless measures against Bani Hashim, were committed to writing by an idolater, Bagheed bin 'Amir bin Hashim and then suspended in Al-Ka'bah. The Prophet (Peace be upon him) invoked Allâh's imprecations upon Bagheed, whose hand was later paralysed. Abu Talib wisely and quietly took stock of the situation and decided to withdraw to a valley on the eastern outskirts of Makkah. Banu Hashim and Banu Al-Muttalib, who followed suit, were thus confined within a narrow pass (Shi'b of Abu Talib), from the beginning of Muharram, the seventh year of Muhammad's mission till the tenth year, viz., a period of three years. It was a stifling siege. The supply of food was almost stopped and the people in confinement faced great hardships.

The idolaters used to buy whatever food commodities entered Makkah lest they should leak to the people in Ash-Shi'b, who were so overstrained that they had to eat leaves of trees and skins of animals. Cries of little children suffering from hunger used to be heard clearly. Nothing to eat reached them except, on few occasions, some meagre quantities of food were smuggled by some compassionate Makkans. During 'the prohibited months' — when hostilities traditionally ceased, they would leave their confinement and buy food coming from outside Makkah. Even then, the food stuff was unjustly overpriced so that their financial situation would fall short of finding access to it.

Hakeem bin Hizam was once on his way to smuggle some wheat to his aunt Khadijah (May Allah be pleased with her) when Abu Jahl intercepted and wanted to debar him. Only when Al-Bukhtari intervened, did Hakeem manage to reach his destination. Abu Talib was so much concerned about the personal safety of his nephew. Whenever people retired to sleep, he would ask the Prophet (Peace be upon him) to lie in his place, but when all the others fell asleep, he would order him to change his place and take another, all of which in an attempt to trick a potential assassin.

Despite all odds, Muhammad (Peace be upon him) persisted in his line and his determination and courage never weakened. He continued to go to Al-Ka'bah and to pray publicly. He used every opportunity to preach to outsiders who visited Makkah for business or on pilgrimage during the sacred months and special seasons of assemblies. This situation ultimately created dissension amongst the various Makkan factions, who were tied with the besieged people by blood relations. After three years of blockade and in Muharram, the tenth year of Muhammad's mission, the pact was broken. Hisham bin 'Amr, who used to smuggle some food to Bani Hashim secretly at night, went to see Zuhair bin Abi Omaiyah Al-Makhzoumy and reproached him for resigning to that intolerable treatment meted out to his uncles in exile. The latter pleaded impotence, but agreed to work with Hisham and form a pressure group that would secure the extrication of the exiles.

On the ground of motivation by uterine relations, there emerged a group of five people who set out to abrogate the pact and declare all relevant clauses null and void. They were Hisham bin 'Amr, Zuhair bin Abi Omaiya, Al-Mut'im bin 'Adi, Abu Al-Bukhtari and Zam'a bin Al-Aswad. They decided to meet in their assembly place and start their self-charged mission from the very precinct of the Sacred House. Zuhair, after circumambulating seven times, along with his colleagues approached the hosts of people there and rebuked them for indulging in the amenities of life whereas their kith and kin of Bani Hashim were perishing on account of starvation and economic boycott. They swore they would never relent until the parchment of boycott was torn to piece and the pact broken at once. Abu Jahl, standing nearby, retorted that it would never be torn.

Zam'a was infuriated and accused Abu Jahl of telling lies, adding that the pact was established and the parchment was written without seeking their approval. Al-Bukhtari intervened and backed Zam'a. Al-Mut'im bin 'Adi and Hisham bin 'Amr attested to the truthfulness of their two companions. Abu Jahl, with a cunning attempt to liquidate the hot argument that was running counter to his malicious goals, answered that the issue had already been resolved sometime and somewhere before.

Abu Talib meanwhile was sitting in a corner of the Mosque. He came to communicate to them that a Revelation had been sent to his nephew, the Prophet (Peace be upon him) to the effect that ants had eaten away all their proclamation that smacked of injustice and aggression except those parts that bore the Name of Allâh. He contended that he would be ready to give Muhammad (Peace be upon him) up to them if his words proved untrue, otherwise, they would have to recant and repeal their boycott.

The Makkans agreed to the soundness of his proposition. Al-Mut'im went to see the parchment and there he did discover that it was eaten away by ants and nothing was left save the part bearing (in the Name of Allâh).

The proclamation was thus abrogated, and Muhammad (Peace be upon him) and the other people were permitted to leave Ash-Sh'ib and return home. In the context of this trial to which the Muslims were subjected, the polytheists had a golden opportunity to experience a striking sign of Muhammad's Prophethood (the white ants eating away the parchment) but to their miserable lot they desisted and augmented in disbelief: "But if they see a Sign, they turn away, and say 'This is continuous magic." [54:2]

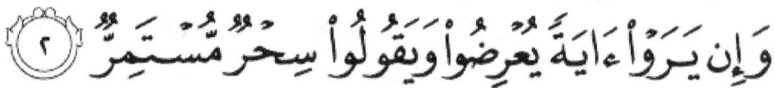

THE FINAL PHASE OF THE DIPLOMACY OF NEGOTIATION:

The Messenger of Allâh (Peace be upon him) left his confinement and went on preaching his Faith as usual. Quraish, likewise, repealed the boycott but went on in their atrocities and oppression on the Muslims. Abu Talib, the octogenarian notable, was still keen on shielding his nephew but by that time, and on account of the series of tremendous events and continual pains, he began to develop certain fits of weakness. No sooner had he emerged victorious from the inhuman boycott, than he was caught in a persistent illness and physical enervation. The polytheists of Makkah, seeing this serious situation and fearing that the stain of infamy that the other Arabs could attribute to them in case they took any aggressive action against the Prophet (Peace be upon him) after he had lost his main support, Abu Talib, took a decision to negotiate with the Prophet (Peace be upon him) once more and submit some concessions withheld previously. They then delegated some representatives to see Abu Talib and discuss the issue with him. Ibn Ishaq and others related: "When a serious illness caught Abu Talib, the people of Quraish began to deliberate on the situation and reviewed the main features that characterized that period and which included the conversion of 'Umar and Hamzah to Islam, coupled with the tremendous stir that Muhammad (Peace be upon him) had created amongst all the tribes of Quraish.

They then deemed it imperative to see Abu Talib before he died to pressure his nephew to negotiate a compromise on the various disputed points. They were afraid that the other Arabs might attribute to them the charge of opportunism."

The delegation of Quraish comprised 25 men including notables like 'Utbah bin Rabi'a, Shaibah bin Rabi'a, Abu Jahl bin Hisham, Omaiyah bin Khalaf, Abu Sufyan bin Harb. They first paid tribute to him and confirmed their high esteem of his person and position among them. They then shifted to the newgive-and-take policy that they claimed they wanted to follow. To substantiate their argument they alleged that they would refrain from intervening in his religion if he did the same. Abu Talib summoned his nephew and apprised him of the minutes of his meeting with them, and said: "Well, my nephew, here are the celebrities of your people. They have proposed this meeting to submit a policy of mutual concessions and peaceful coexistence." The Messenger of Allâh (Peace be upon him) turned to them saying: "I will guide you to the means by which you will gain sovereignty over both the Arabs and non- Arabs."

In another version, the Prophet (Peace be upon him) addressed Abu Talib in the following words: "O uncle! Why don't you call them unto something better?" Abu Talib asked him, "What is it that you invite them to?" The Prophet (Peace be upon him) replied, "I invite them to hold fast to a Message that is bound to give them access to kingship over the Arabs and non-Arabs." According to Ibn Ishaq's version, "It is just one word that will give you supremacy over the Arabs and non-Arabs." The Makkan deputies were taken by incredible surprise and began to wonder what sort of word was that which would benefit them to that extent. Abu Jahl asked, "What is that word? I swear by your father that we will surely grant you your wish followed by ten times as much." He said, "I want you to testify that there is no god worthy to be worshipped but Allâh, and then divest yourselves of any sort of worship you harbour for any deities other than Allâh." They immediately clapped their hands in ridicule, and said "How can you expect us to combine all the deities in one God. It is really something incredible." On their way out leaving, they said to one another, "By god this man [Muhammad (Peace be upon him)] will never relent, nor will he offer any concessions.

Let us hold fast to the religion of our forefathers, and Allâh will in due course adjudicate and settle the dispute between us and him." As regards this incident, Allâh revealed the following verses: "Sâd: [These letters (Sâd, etc.) are one of the miracles of the Qur'ân and none but Allâh (Alone) knows their meanings]. By the Qur'ân full of reminding. Nay, those who disbelieve are in false pride and Apposition. How many a generation We have destroyed before them, and they cried out when there was no longer time for escape! And they (Arab pagans) wonder that a warner [Prophet Muhammad (Peace be upon him)] has come to them from among themselves! And the disbelievers say: 'This [Prophet Muhammad (Peace be upon him)] is a sorcerer, a liar. Has he made the gods (all) into One God (Allâh). Verily, this is a curious thing!' And the leaders among them went about (saying): 'Go on, and remain constant to your gods! Verily, this is a thing designed (against you)! We have not heard (the like) of this among the people of these later days. This is nothing but an invention.'" [38:1-7]

صٓ وَٱلْقُرْءَانِ ذِى ٱلذِّكْرِ ۝

بَلِ ٱلَّذِينَ كَفَرُوا۟ فِى عِزَّةٍ وَشِقَاقٍ ۝

كَمْ أَهْلَكْنَا مِن قَبْلِهِم مِّن قَرْنٍ فَنَادَوا۟ وَّلَاتَ حِينَ مَنَاصٍ ۝

وَعَجِبُوٓا۟ أَن جَآءَهُم مُّنذِرٌ مِّنْهُمْ ۖ وَقَالَ ٱلْكَٰفِرُونَ هَٰذَا سَٰحِرٌ كَذَّابٌ ۝

أَجَعَلَ ٱلْءَالِهَةَ إِلَٰهًا وَٰحِدًا ۖ إِنَّ هَٰذَا لَشَىْءٌ عُجَابٌ ۝

وَٱنطَلَقَ ٱلْمَلَأُ مِنْهُمْ أَنِ ٱمْشُوا۟ وَٱصْبِرُوا۟ عَلَىٰٓ ءَالِهَتِكُمْ ۖ إِنَّ هَٰذَا لَشَىْءٌ يُرَادُ ۝

مَا سَمِعْنَا بِهَٰذَا فِى ٱلْمِلَّةِ ٱلْءَاخِرَةِ إِنْ هَٰذَآ إِلَّا ٱخْتِلَٰقٌ ۝

Islamic quotes

"The crying of the sinners is more loved to Allah than the tasbeeh of the arrogant."

"When you do not have knowledge someone can bring you dirt and you will believe it is gold."

"A persons' tongue can give you the taste of His heart."

"Patience is when the heart doesn't lament and the mouth doesn't complain."
—

"If scholars are wicked and worshippers are ignorant, the trial will be severe."
—

"There is nothing more beneficial to the heart than reciting the Quran."

"Many ignorant people rely upon Allah's mercy and forgiveness yet forget that He is also severe in punishment."

"A deprivation of a few moments [of pleasure] is better than permanent regret."

"Satisfaction is when a person submits himself to his Lord."

"Allah will never humiliate one who takes his Lord as a friend and protector."

"Indeed the Believer who has reliance upon Allah, if the creation plot against him, Allah plots for him on his behalf and brings about victory for him, without any effort or strength from himself."

"Who sincerely relies on Allah to achieve something, will achieve it."

"Misdeeds stand as a block for earning. Surely, one can be deprived of provision by committing sins."

"Knowledge is not about narrating a lot but it is about Taqwa (piety)."

"If you knew Allah as He should be known, you would leave people aside and take Him as your Companion."

"Allah is displeased when you stop asking him and mankind is displeased when asked."

"O you who are patient! Bear a little more, just a little more remains."

"If the human knew the pleasure of meeting Allah and being near to him, then he (human) would feel grief for being distant from him (Allah)."

"All hard work is easy for the believers when they understand that Allah hears them."

"Allah promised you the pleasures of the Hereafter, so do not be in a hurry and seek them in this worldly life as if you are cutting plants before their harvest time, while they are much better if you wait. Likewise, the pleasures of the Hereafter are so much better."

"Our life in this world is like that of a harvest field. What you plant here is what you will eat in the hereafter."

"Be to Allah as He wishes, and He will be to you more than you can wish for."

"Allah loves from his slave that he beautifies his tongue with the truth, and his heart with Ikhlaas and love, turning repentantly and reliance upon Allah."

"A sign of well-being and success is that when one increases in knowledge, he becomes more humble and merciful."

"It is a punishment for a sinner, indulging in sins, to eventually be forgotten by Allah and left alone with devil."

"The sincere person has humility for Allah alone and hope in him alone, requesting from him alone."

"The soul will never become pious and purified except through undergoing afflictions. It is the same as gold that can never be pure except after removing all the base metals in it."

"The people of Quran are those who read it and act upon it, even if they have not memorized it."

"Whoever wrongs you and then comes in order to apologize then you should accept his apology out of humbleness and leave his intention up to Allah, exalted is He."

"O people who take pleasure in a life that will disappear; falling in love with a fading shadow is pure stupidity."

"Knowledge is a carpet, none treads upon it except for the one near (to Allah)."

"Love is a spring well that does not dry up. Its purity and sweetness increases when it is for the sake of Allah and in the way of Allah."

"The best of those who fast are the ones who fast who are more plentiful in the (legislated) Dhikr (remembrance) of Allah, the mighty and majestic, during their fast."

"If Allah wills goodness for a slave, he would prevent him from feeling good about his deeds and from telling others about them, and would busy him with thinking about his sins, and he will continue to be like this until he enters Paradise."

"The sinner does not feel any remorse over his sins. That is because his heart is already dead."

"A real man is the one who fears the death of his heart, not his body."

"Whenever sins increase, loneliness/gloom intensifies."

"When Allah is with you, then all worries, grief and sadness disappear; no grief can remain when Allah is with the slave."

"Wasting time is worse than death, because death separates you from this world whereas wasting time separates you from Allah."

"And the servant; if he exchanges disobedience with obedience, Allah will exchange the punishment upon him with pardoning (him), and humiliation with honor."

"Whoever desires to purify his heart, then let him prefer Allah to his desires."

"Perhaps you might me asleep while the doors of heaven are knocking with tens of supplications for you, by a poor person you aided, or a sad person you cheered up or a distressed person you brought relief to. Therefore don't underestimate doing good at all."

"If Allah the exalted, forgave a woman who gave water to a thirsty dog, what would he do the one who gives water to the thirsty, food to the hungry and dress to those Muslims who don't have clothes."

"Your nafs is just like your enemy, once it finds you serious, it obeys you. If it finds weakness from you, It will take you as prisoner."

"Every type of knowledge and action which doesn't increase the strength of imaan and yaqeen has been corrupted."

"For the person who repents and becomes better after a sin, the sin is a mercy."

"Whoever thinks of the greatness of Allah will never be at ease in committing wrong actions."

"Sitting with the poor and less fortunate people removes the ego and pride from your heart." –

"It is enough of an honor for you that you are His(Allah's) worshipper, and it is sufficient glory for you that He(Allah) is your Lord."

"Whoever wants to purify his heart, must prefer Allah over and above his own desires."

"As long as you pray, you knock on the door of Allah. And whoever knocks at the door of Allah, He will open it for him."

"Sins destroy the heart the same way poison destroys the body."

"Sins need to be burnt, either with the pain of regret in this world, or with the fire of hell in the Hereafter!"

"In the heart there is a void that can only be filled by loving Allah."

"If Allah wants well for a slave, He strips away from his heart the ability to see his own good deeds and speaking about them with his tongue, and preoccupies him with seeing his own sin, and it continues to remain in front of his eyes until he enters jannah."

"The servant of Allah who seeks the pleasure of Allah never abandons tawbah (repentance)."

"The intelligent person does not cling to this material world."

"Allah is displeased when you stop asking of Him and mankind is displeased when asked."

"The lover of the world cannot get rid from three things –

1. Constant worry
2. Permanent discomfort
3. Relentless distress."

"And when the eye no longer cries out of fear of Allaah, know that this drought originates from the hardness of the heart."

"Know the value of what was lost, and cry like someone who knows the value of what has passed him by."

"If the heart becomes hardened – the eye becomes dry."

"Dhikr is a tree with fruits of awareness. The more frequent dhikr is made, the stronger the roots of a tree and more fruits on it."

"Sins generate more sins, and one leads to another, until they overpower a man and he finds it difficult to repent from that. As one of the earlier generation said: One of the punishments of bad deeds is more bad deeds, and one of the rewards of good deeds is more good deeds."

"Satisfaction is when a person submits himself to his Lord (Allah)."

"Sinning will leave you poor and regretful."

"Some people remain deprived of knowledge due to their poor ability to remain silent."

"Allah created both paradise and hellfire for the sinners. Hellfire is for the sinner who sinned but didn't ask Allah for forgiveness. But paradise is for the sinner who sinned but turned to Allah and asked for his forgiveness."

"Deeds without sincerity are like a traveler who carries in his water jug dirt. The carrying of its burden him and it brings no benefit."

"This Dunya(world) is just like shadow, If you try to catch it, you will never be able to do so. But if you turn your back towards it, it has no choice but to follow you."

"Corruption of character arises from putting the creation between yourself and Allah, and by putting your ego between yourself and his creation."

"Don't carry anxiety for the future because it is in the hands of Allah."

"If a heart becomes attached to anything other than Allah, Allah makes him dependent on what he is attached to. And he will be betrayed by it."

"Friday is the balance of the week, Ramadan is the valance of the year and hajj is the balance of the life."

"Falling in love is a disease and its cure is to marry the one you love."

"When you make du'a it is a sign that Allah loves you and has intended good for you."

"When Allah tests you, it is never intended to destroy you. When He removes something in your possession, it is only in order to empty your hands for an even greater gift."

"Know the value of what was lost, and cry like someone who knows the value of what has passed him by."

"Undoubtedly, one should never please people by displeasing Allah."

"The heart gets sick as the body does and its cure is in asking for forgiveness and protection. It also becomes rusty like a mirror does and it is polished by remembering Allah. The heart can also be naked like the body and can lose its dress and decoration, which is piety.And it can feel hunger and thirst like the body does, and its nourishment is knowledge, love, trust, and offering service to Allah."

Good Books

Search by **ISBN** to buy the correct book

Stories of the Prophets	ISBN: 9781643543888
Story of the Holy Prophet	ISBN: 9781643544267
The Noble Quran (Arabic)	ISBN: 9781643543994
Koran (English: Easy to Read)	ISBN: 9781643540924
Life in al-Barzakh: Life after Death	ISBN: 9781643544144
The Heavenly Dispute	ISBN: 9781643544168
The Journey of the Strangers	ISBN: 9781643544175
Disciplining the Soul	ISBN: 9781643544151

ISBN: 9781643544120

Diseases of the Hearts & Cures	ISBN 9781643544106
The Friends of Allah	ISBN: 9781643544236
The Path to Guidance	ISBN: 9781643544052
Miracles of the Prophet	ISBN: 9781643544038
Seerah of Prophet Muhammad	ISBN: 9781643543222
Book on Islam and Marriage	ISBN: 9781073877140
The Spiritual Cure	ISBN: 9781643544212
Great Women of Islam	ISBN: 9781643543758
Stories of the Koran	ISBN: 9781095900796
The Purification of the Soul	ISBN: 9781643541389
Al-Fawaid: Wise Sayings	ISBN: 9781727812718
The Book of Hajj	ISBN: 9781072243335

40 Hadith Qudsi	ISBN: 9781070655949
40 Hadith Nawawi	ISBN: 9781070547428
The Legacy of the Prophet	ISBN: 9781080249343
The Ideal Muslim Woman	ISBN: 9781643543192
The Soul's Journey after Death	ISBN: 9781643541365
Khalid Bin Al-Waleed	ISBN: 9781643543420
The Islamic View of Jesus	ISBN: 978164354335
Don't Be Sad	ISBN: 9781643543451
Ota Benga	ISBN: 9798698096665

www.ingramcontent.com/pod-product-compliance
Lightning Source LLC
Chambersburg PA
CBHW081401070526
44583CB00020B/2634